Caesar's *Gallic War*

OKLAHOMA SERIES IN CLASSICAL CULTURE

Oklahoma Series in Classical Culture

Caesar's

GALLIC WAR

A Commentary

HERBERT W. BENARIO

UNIVERSITY OF OKLAHOMA PRESS

Norman

Library of Congress Cataloging-in-Publication Data

Benario, Herbert W.
    Caesar's Gallic war : a commentary / Herbert W. Benario.
      p. cm. — (Oklahoma series in classical culture v. 46)
    Includes index.
    ISBN 978-0-8061-4252-4 (pbk. : alk. paper)   1. Caesar, Julius. De bello
Gallico   2. Latin language—Glossaries, vocabularies, etc.   3. Gaul—
History—Gallic Wars, 58–51 B.C.   I. Title.   II. Title: Julius Caesar's Gallic
war.
    PA6246.B46 2012
    878'.01—dc23

2011044203

Caesar's Gallic War: A Commentary is Volume 46 in the Oklahoma
Series in Classical Culture.

The paper in this book meets the guidelines for permanence
and durability of the Committee on Production Guidelines for Book
Longevity of the Council on Library Resources, Inc. ∞

CONTENTS

ILLUSTRATIONS

PREFACE

For many generations of Latin students, the second year of study was the stronghold of Julius Caesar's *Gallic War*. This was the first work read in its original form. Over time, however, particularly in recent decades, Caesar faded from Latin curricula, both because of new approaches to teaching Latin and the understanding that warfare in antiquity was not of much interest to many youngsters, particularly young women.

With the change in the Advanced Placement Latin program, which goes into effect in autumn 2012, Caesar has returned. He will be half of the sole Latin AP exam, and interest in the greatest work of one of Rome's most extraordinary figures will be once again in the forefront. The present volume aims to guide and assist in that enterprise. It may also be useful in lower-level college courses. The innate interest of Caesar's narrative, such as the first invasion of Britain and the description of the druids, will appeal to most students of Latin.

In winter 2010 I was asked by John Drayton, the Classics Editor of the University of Oklahoma Press, if I would be interested in preparing a text for the new program. I agreed to do so, but no information about the character and contents of the new AP program would be made public until late June.

When Mr. Drayton retired in the spring of 2010, his successor was Alessandra Jacobi Tamulevich. I am grateful to both for their advice and encouragement, guiding me through the various stages of publication.

I am also grateful to two friends of long standing in Atlanta, both retired secondary-school teachers of remarkable abilities and effect upon students. They are Mrs. Lynne McClendon and Mrs. Elizabeth Frank, who were kind enough to read my notes at an early stage and point out deficiencies and possible improvements. I also profited from the comments of the Press' two readers.

The most difficult task for me was the construction of the

Vocabulary. I express deep gratitude to Professor Richard La-
Fleur of the University of Georgia for allowing me to use a vocabulary which he had prepared for one of his books and to Miss
Alexandra Mina, a Classics major in Emory College, for her
careful and meticulous analysis of all Caesar's words in the *Se-
lections*. She indicated which words were in the Vocabulary and
which I needed to add. Both Professor LaFleur and Miss Mina
saved me from much tedious labor. Any serious reader of the
Bellum Gallicum will have at hand two aged but still great
commentaries on the work, by T. Rice Holmes, *C. Iuli Caesaris
Commentarii Rerum in Gallia Gestarum VII, A. Hirti Commentarius VIII* (Oxford 1914), and Heinrich Meusel, *Commentarii de Bello Gallico*, 19th ed. (Berlin 1961). I have had frequent
recourse to both.

Emory University, as always, was very supportive of my la-
bors, particularly the Department of Classics. But the greatest
support came from a Heilbrun Fellowship awarded me for the
academic year 2010–2011 by the University's Emeritus College.
For all this, I express my deepest appreciation.

But the *ultima laus* must go to my wife, who has been the
dedicatee of all my books. Once more I am delighted to inscribe,

Cui dono lepidum novum libellum?
Janicae, tibi.

Atlanta
July 2011

Introduction

Julius Caesar. Museo della Civiltà Romana, Rome. (Photograph by H. W. Benario)

THE HISTORY OF ROME AND THE GAULS FROM THE FOURTH CENTURY TO CAESAR'S TIME

Northern Italy was a melting pot of Etruscans and Celts into the fourth century B.C. The Po valley, with its easy transport and fertile soil, had attracted Gallic tribes over the Alps to such an extent that the north of Italy became known as Gallia Cisalpina, Gaul this side of the Alps. At the beginning of the fourth century, some Gallic tribes were emboldened to cross the Appennine Mountains, which run like a spine down the center of the Italian peninsula: they even sacked Rome in the year 390 (a date now generally changed to 387). The Gauls occupied the city for nine months; the Capitol was saved by the cackling of Juno's sacred geese, in one of Rome's best-known stories. The siege ended only after the Romans paid an enormous tribute in gold. This sad episode in Rome's history is vividly described by Livy, in his history *Ab urbe condita*, at the end of book 5.

Gallic incursions continued through the fourth century into the third. The last invasion was in 225, which the Romans decisively crushed. Determined to end these recurring incursions, the Romans conquered northern Italy within a few years. They then faced the enormous threat of Hannibal in the Second Punic War (218–201), in the course of which they obtained control of a substantial part of Spain. Much of the second century was spent in consolidating this territory; Roman armies needed to pass through southern Gaul to reach Spain. A settlement of this problem was finally obtained in the last quarter of the century, when Rome aided the Greek city of Massilia (now Marseille) against neighboring tribes and then established the Provincia (now Provence) in the year 121. The province's capital was the city of Narbo (Narbonne), founded three years later.

The next crisis followed very soon. The Germanic tribes of the Cimbri and Teutones, whose homes were in Denmark and vicinity, had begun a long journey to the western lands seeking new homes. When they at the last entered Gallic territory, they found considerable support from local tribes when they were first met by Roman armies. In the course of less than a decade, they defeated five consular armies. Only after Gaius Marius had been elected to five consecutive consulships and had transformed the Roman armies were the Germans defeated in two overwhelming battles in 102 and 101.

For the next forty years, Gaul settled into a generally peaceful existence. The German tribes, indeed, on the other side of the Rhine were always a threat; in general, however, there was a *modus vivendi* among them. This was the situation in Gaul when Caesar became *proconsul* in 58.

Roman coin stamped with Caesar's image

CAESAR'S LIFE AND CAREER

Gaius Iulius Caesar was born in the year 100 B.C. He traced his ancestry back to the goddess Venus, as she was the mother of Aeneas, the founder of the Roman people after he had led the survivors of the Trojan War to Italy. Aeneas' son was Iulus, whose name furnishes the link for Caesar's claim of "divine" ancestry. The first twenty years of Caesar's life were marked by the political rivalry of Marius and of Sulla, which led to civil war and the dictatorship of Sulla.

Although Caesar was a patrician by birth, his family was connected to that of Marius, a *popularis*, a relationship which led to difficult times when Sulla, an optimate, controlled the state. When Caesar was thirty-one years old, he delivered the funeral oration honoring the widow of Marius, his aunt Julia, which brought him glory and enmity simultaneously, for he displayed Marius' *imago*, seen in public for the first time since the death of Sulla.

After Sulla's resignation from the dictatorship in 79, the decade of the seventies was increasingly dominated by Gnaeus Pompeius Magnus (Pompey the Great) and M. Licinius Crassus, the wealthiest man in Rome. Caesar was elected *quaestor* for the years 69 and 68, *curulis aedilis* for 65, and *praetor* for 62. The year before, however, he had, to the surprise of many, by means of extensive bribery, been elected *pontifex maximus* for life, thereby becoming the head of the Roman state religion.

After his praetorship, he was assigned the province of Further Spain, probably with the title of *proconsul*. This province proved to be doubly important. He waged wars and thereby honed his innate military skills and developed a relationship with his troops, above all with the Tenth Legion, which stood him in good stead for the remainder of his life. He also was able, as many governors were, to become a wealthy man by draining the resources of the province.

In 60, he entered into a private alliance with Pompey and Crassus, which became known as the First Triumvirate, to satisfy the needs of all three for glory and political security. Caesar was elected consul for 59 with Marcus Calpurnius Bibulus as colleague, who attempted to thwart Caesar's legislation by any and all means, all of which Caesar ignored to such a degree that the year became identified as the "consulship of Julius and Caesar." He was allotted the provinces of Cisalpine Gaul and Illyricum, which bordered the eastern side of the Adriatic Sea, for 58 and soon thereafter Transalpine Gaul was added. When he left Rome for his provinces, he had command of a total of four legions; as the years and his campaigns passed, he raised seven more, for a total of eleven.

His command and warfare in Gaul ended with the year 51. The next years focused upon the rivalry of Caesar and Pompey (Crassus now being dead), which ultimately led to civil war. This lasted approximately two years and ended with Caesar's victory at Pharsalus in 48. Although warfare continued for several more years against Pompey's family and allies, Caesar dominated the state. He was elected consul four more times and dictator four times before being designated *dictator perpetuus*. In the autumn of 46 he celebrated four magnificent triumphs in rapid succession, honoring his successes in Gaul, Egypt, Asia Minor, and Africa.

Because by law the term of a dictator was limited to six months, a permanent dictatorship seemed to many of the senatorial order a return to the days of the monarchy, and on March 15, 44, the Ides of March, Caesar was assassinated by a group led by Brutus and Cassius.

> then burst his mighty heart;
> And, in his mantle muffling up his face,
> Even at the base of Pompey's statue,
> Which all the while ran blood, great Caesar fell.
>
> Shakespeare, *Julius Caesar*, 3.2.191–194

THE NATURE OF THE WORK
AND CAESAR'S STYLE

The *Bellum Gallicum* is called *commentarii*, not *historia* or *res gestae*. If Caesar himself chose the name, it was a clear indicator that he had not set out to write "history," which by ancient definition involved careful stylistic characteristics, but that he intended his work to serve as raw material for someone else to apply the ultimate polish. *Res gestae* is the normal expression for one's achievements. The most significant example of the use of that expression is in the title of the emperor Augustus' very lengthy delineation of all he had done for the state. This was inscribed on the walls of the Temple of Rome and Augustus in Ancyra (later Angora, now Ankara, Turkey) and began, in large letters, RES GESTAE DIVI AVGVSTI. Augustus, however, used the first person constantly when referring to himself; Caesar in his commentaries had determined to separate his subject from the writer by referring to himself in the third person, a device that suggests greater objectivity.

Aulus Hirtius, an officer under Caesar in the latter stages of the Gallic War, composed book 8 to complete the record of the war. In his preface, he writes, *Caesaris nostri commentarios rerum gestarum Galliae . . . contexui . . . qui sunt editi, ne scientia tantarum rerum scriptoribus desit* ("I have woven together our Caesar's *commentarii* of his achievements in Gaul; these have been published lest the knowledge of such great events be unavailable to writers"). *Commentarii*, then, furnish the raw material of deeds and events with which another writer can produce an appropriate history. That, however, never happened, because Caesar's simple elegance and brevity of style were considered too great a challenge. Cicero commented upon this in his rhetorical work *Brutus*, written in the year 46. A significant problem in assessing the *Bellum Gallicum* lies in determining when Caesar wrote each book and when the books were each or all published. Did he write each book in winter, in his provincial headquarters, recounting the past year's activities and campaigns, and then publish each individually? Or did he write the entire work, in a continuous burst of energy, in the winter of 52–51, after the defeat of Vercingetorix at Alesia, and publish the whole that winter or the following spring?

I propose a third alternative, that he wrote each winter and ultimately, when the war appeared over, published the whole. His victory at Alesia increased his prestige and *auctoritas* among the Senate at Rome and the Roman people in general. The triumph which he was awarded, in which Vercingetorix was the prize display, although delayed a few years, was one of the most glorious and stupendous such events in Rome's history.

Had Caesar waited until the late 50s to write the whole, the vividness of each year's events would have largely faded, and many events would have begun to flow together. The detail which Caesar presents with great consistency, to my mind, supports the view of annual composition.

Why Caesar chose to write the *Bellum Gallicum* with reference to himself in the third person we do not know. No surviving earlier text of Latin literature reveals an author doing so. Caesar may have made this choice for the shock value that a reader would at first feel and to win a greater sense of objectivity. The entire work has only one instance where Caesar refers to himself in the first person.

Because this was Caesar's regular practice and he generally refers to a third person object, the possibility of confusion with phrases and clauses is very real. Word order and word position can be crucial, and one must be alert to use of reflexives and demonstratives. Consider this sentence: "Caesar conquered the Gallic chieftain with his men." Is the phrase "with his men" an ablative of means referring to Caesar, or an ablative of accompaniment referring to the chieftain? In the former instance, we must expect *suis viris*, in the latter *eius viris*. When there is a subordinate clause, the reflexive may either refer to the subject of its own clause or, if the clause presents the actual words or thoughts of the subject of the main clause, to that subject. This usage is known as an indirect reflexive.

Speeches are a staple of ancient historiography. They often stem from the historian's knowledge of events and circumstances and his own imagination. Rare must have been the occasion when the historian himself heard the address delivered or could speak to someone who had been present, or even had been the orator. Thucydides might well have heard Pericles' funeral oration in Athens in 429 B.C., and Tacitus certainly learned from his father-in-law, Agricola, what had been said by him and others in the Roman wars in Britain in A.D. 77–84.

Caesar knew what he had said when he addressed his troops. He could learn from his subordinates what they had said in similar circumstances. But he could only guess what had been appropriate for an enemy chieftain to say in particular circumstances. Indirect speech is therefore in most instances preferable, as it suggests what X might well have said, rather than implying that the words of a direct speech were precise. In the first three books of the *Bellum Gallicum* there is no direct speech; in the later books there are two, in 4.25 and 5.30. Each presents a statement by an officer of noble and bold sentiments, which represent the Roman army at its best. Caesar evidently wished to immortalize these two men.

SUGGESTED READING

Adcock, F. E. *Caesar as Man of Letters*. Cambridge, 1956.
Cambridge Ancient History, 2nd ed., vol. 9. Cambridge, 1994.
———. Chapter 9, "The Senate and the *populares*, 69–60 B.C.," 327–367. By T. P. Wiseman.
———. Chapter 10, "Caesar, Pompey and Rome, 59–50 B.C.," 368–423. By T. P. Wiseman.
———. Chapter 11, "Caesar: Civil War and Dictatorship," 424–467. By Elizabeth Rawson.
———. Chapter 12, "The Aftermath of the Ides," 468–490. By Elizabeth Rawson.
Gelzer, M. *Caesar: Politician and Statesman*. Oxford, 1968.
Green, M. J. *The World of the Druids*. New York. 1997.
Griffin, M. T., ed. *A Companion to Julius Caesar*. Malden, Mass., 2009.
Gruen, E. S. *The Last Generation of the Roman Republic*. Berkeley and Los Angeles, 1974.
Hadas, M., ed. and trans. *The Gallic War and Other Writings by Julius Caesar*. New York, 1957.
Holmes, T. R. E. *Caesar's Conquest of Gaul*. Oxford, 1899; 2nd ed. 1911.
———. *Ancient Britain and the Invasions of Julius Caesar*. Oxford, 1907.
———. *C. Iuli Caesaris commentarii rerum in Gallia gestarum VII. A. Hirtii commentarius VIII*. Oxford, 1914.
Meier, C. *Caesar: A Biography*. London, 1996.
Napoleon III, Emperor of France. *History of Julius Caesar*. 2 vols. New York, 1865–1866.
Salway, P. *Roman Britain*. Oxford, 1984.
Southern, P. *Julius Caesar*. Charleston, S.C., 2001.
Wiseman, A., and P. Wiseman, eds. and trans. *Julius Caesar: The Battle for Gaul*. Boston, 1980.

RHETORICAL AND
GRAMMATICAL TERMS

alliteration   use of two or more words in close proximity that begin with the same letter or sound.

anaphora   repetition of a word at the beginning of two or more clauses.

assonance   the repetition of the same or similar vowel sounds.

asyndeton   omission of connectives in a series.

chiasmus   reversal of the order of words from one phrase to a second, such as noun, adjective, adjective, noun, or nominative, accusative, accusative, nominative. The order is *a,b,b,a*.

ellipsis   omission of a word or words, the sense of which is nonetheless understood.

hendiadys   expression of an idea through two coordinated nouns rather than by one noun limited either by an adjective or by another noun in a different case.

inconcinnity   avoidance of parallel constructions.

juxtaposition   proximity of words, often for comparison or contrast.

litotes   emphasis of a word or statement by denial of its opposite.

onomatopoeia   choice of a word which, by its sound, gives a sense of the word's meaning.

periphrasis   circumlocution, which avoids the necessity of saying something directly.

pleonasm   redundancy of expression.

synchysis   interlocked word order, with similar parts of speech or parallel cases or ideas appearing in the order *a,b,a,b*.

tricolon   three closely linked words or expressions in the same construction.

zeugma   use of a word with two or more others, with only one of which it has a precise relationship.

ablative and accusative supine   the former, ending in –*u*, is an ablative of specification; the latter, ending in –*um*, is used to express purpose.

dative of agent   used most commonly with the gerundive, to indicate the person or persons responsible for the action.

dative of purpose   often used with another dative, to indicate the purpose or effect upon the persons or circumstance mentioned in the other dative.

gerund and gerundive of purpose the gerundive use is probably more common; choice of one or the other often depends upon sound; for example, *ad urbem delendam* is preferable to *ad urbem delendum*.

implied indirect discourse the use of accusative and infinitive to express speech or thought, even though no verb of speech or thought is present.

objective genitive occurs when the noun or adjective upon which the genitive depends has a verbal sense.

partitive genitive the genitive represents the whole of which the noun on which it depends refers to a part.

relative clause of purpose clause introduced by a relative pronoun or relative adverb (such as *ubi*), rather than by *ut* or *ne*.

Text and Commentary

C. IVLI CAESARIS DE BELLO GALLICO COMMENTARIORVM

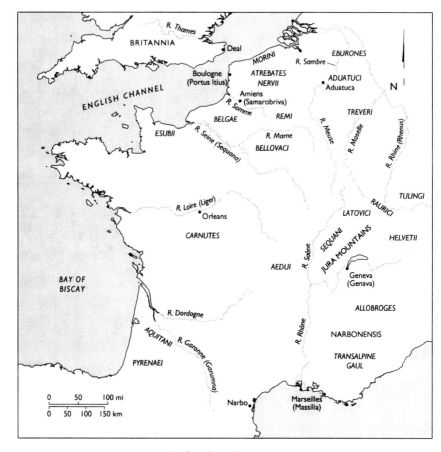

Gaul and southern Britain

LIBER PRIMVS I–VII

1. GALLIA est omnis divisa in partis tris, quarum unam
incolunt Belgae, aliam Aquitani, tertiam qui ipsorum lingua
Celtae, nostra Galli appellantur. Hi omnes lingua, institutis, legibus inter se differunt. Gallos ab Aquitanis
Garumna flumen, a Belgis Matrona et Sequana dividit. 5
Horum omnium fortissimi sunt Belgae, propterea quod
a cultu atque humanitate provinciae longissime absunt,
minimeque ad eos mercatores saepe commeant atque ea
quae ad effeminandos animos pertinent important, proxi-
mique sunt Germanis qui trans Rhenum incolunt, quibus- 10
cum continenter bellum gerunt. Qua de causa Helvetii
quoque reliquos Gallos virtute praecedunt, quod fere coti-
dianis proeliis cum Germanis contendunt, cum aut suis
finibus eos prohibent aut ipsi in eorum finibus bellum
gerunt. Eorum una pars, quam Gallos obtinere dictum est, 15
initium capit a flumine Rhodano; continetur Garumna
flumine, Oceano, finibus Belgarum; attingit etiam ab
Sequanis et Helvetiis flumen Rhenum; vergit ad septentriones. Belgae ab extremis Galliae finibus oriuntur; pertinent ad inferiorem partem fluminis Rheni; spectant in 20
septentrionem et orientem solem. Aquitania a Garumna
flumine ad Pyrenaeos montis et eam partem Oceani quae
est ad Hispaniam pertinet; spectat inter occasum solis et
septentriones.

2. Apud Helvetios longe nobilissimus fuit et ditissimus
Orgetorix. Is, M. Messalla et M. Pupio Pisone consulibus,
regni cupiditate inductus coniurationem nobilitatis fecit, et
civitati persuasit ut de finibus suis cum omnibus copiis
exirent: perfacile esse, cum virtute omnibus praestarent, 5
totius Galliae imperio potiri. Id hoc facilius eis persuasit,
quod undique loci natura Helvetii continentur: una ex

17

parte flumine Rheno latissimo atque altissimo, qui agrum
Helvetium a Germanis dividit; altera ex parte monte Iura
10 altissimo, qui est inter Sequanos et Helvetios; tertia lacu
Lemanno et flumine Rhodano, qui provinciam nostram ab
Helvetiis dividit. His rebus fiebat ut et minus late
vagarentur et minus facile finitimis bellum inferre possent:
qua ex parte homines bellandi cupidi magno dolore adficie-
15 bantur. Pro multitudine autem hominum et pro gloria
belli atque fortitudinis angustos se finis habere arbitrabantur,
qui in longitudinem milia passuum CCXL, in latitudinem
CLXXX patebant.

3.   His rebus adducti et auctoritate Orgetorigis permoti,
constituerunt ea quae ad proficiscendum pertinerent com-
parare, iumentorum et carrorum quam maximum numerum
coemere, sementis quam maximas facere ut in itinere copia
5 frumenti suppeteret, cum proximis civitatibus pacem et
amicitiam confirmare. Ad eas res conficiendas biennium
sibi satis esse duxerunt: in tertium annum profectionem
lege confirmant. Ad eas res conficiendas Orgetorix deli-
gitur. Is sibi legationem ad civitates suscepit. In eo
10 itinere persuadet Castico Catamantaloedis filio Sequano,
cuius pater regnum in Sequanis multos annos obtinuerat et
a senatu populi Romani amicus appellatus erat, ut regnum
in civitate sua occuparet quod pater ante habuerat; item-
que Dumnorigi Aeduo fratri Diviciaci, qui eo tempore
15 principatum in civitate obtinebat ac maxime plebi acceptus
erat, ut idem conaretur persuadet, eique filiam suam in
matrimonium dat. Perfacile factu esse illis probat conata
perficere, propterea quod ipse suae civitatis imperium
obtenturus esset: non esse dubium quin totius Galliae
20 plurimum Helvetii possent; se suis copiis suoque exercitu
illis regna conciliaturum confirmat. Hac oratione adducti
inter se fidem et ius iurandum dant, et regno occupato per
tris potentissimos ac firmissimos populos totius Galliae sese
potiri posse sperant.

4. Ea res est Helvetiis per indicium enuntiata. Moribus
suis Orgetorigem ex vinclis causam dicere coegerunt. Damnatum poenam sequi oportebat ut igni cremaretur. Die
constituta causae dictionis Orgetorix ad iudicium omnem
suam familiam ad hominum milia decem undique coegit, 5
et omnis clientis obaeratosque suos, quorum magnum
numerum habebat, eodem conduxit: per eos ne causam
diceret se eripuit. Cum civitas ob eam rem incitata
armis ius suum exsequi conaretur, multitudinemque hominum
ex agris magistratus cogerent, Orgetorix mortuus est; neque 10
abest suspicio, ut Helvetii arbitrantur, quin ipse sibi mortem
consciverit.

5. Post eius mortem nihilo minus Helvetii id quod consti-
tuerant facere conantur, ut e finibus suis exeant. Ubi iam
se ad eam rem paratos esse arbitrati sunt, oppida sua
omnia, numero ad duodecim, vicos ad quadringentos,
reliqua privata aedificia incendunt; frumentum omne, 5
praeterquam quod secum portaturi erant, comburunt, ut
domum reditionis spe sublata paratiores ad omnia pericula
subeunda essent; trium mensum molita cibaria sibi quem-
que domo efferre iubent. Persuadent Rauricis et Tulingis
et Latovicis finitimis suis uti eodem usi consilio, oppidis 10
suis vicisque exustis, una cum eis proficiscantur, Boiosque,
qui trans Rhenum incoluerant et in agrum Noricum trans-
ierant Noreiamque oppugnarant, receptos ad se socios sibi
asciscunt.

6. Erant omnino itinera duo, quibus itineribus domo exire
possent: unum per Sequanos, angustum et difficile, inter
montem Iuram et flumen Rhodanum, vix qua singuli
carri ducerentur; mons autem altissimus impendebat, ut
facile perpauci prohibere possent: alterum per provinciam 5
nostram, multo facilius atque expeditius, propterea quod
inter finis Helvetiorum et Allobrogum, qui nuper pacati

erant, Rhodanus fluit, isque non nullis locis vado transitur.
Extremum oppidum Allobrogum est proximumque Helve-
10 tiorum finibus Genava. Ex eo oppido pons ad Helvetios
pertinet. Allobrogibus sese vel persuasuros, quod nondum
bono animo in populum Romanum viderentur, existimabant vel vi coacturos ut per suos finis eos ire pate-
rentur. Omnibus rebus ad profectionem comparatis, diem
15 dicunt, qua die ad ripam Rhodani omnes conveniant. Is
dies erat a. d. V. Kal. April., L. Pisone A. Gabinio consulibus.

7. Caesari cum id nuntiatum esset, eos per provinciam
nostram iter facere conari, maturat ab urbe proficisci, et
quam maximis potest itineribus in Galliam ulteriorem con-
tendit, et ad Genavam pervenit. Provinciae toti quam
5 maximum potest militum numerum imperat (erat omnino
in Gallia ulteriore legio una), pontem qui erat ad Genavam
iubet rescindi. Ubi de eius adventu Helvetii certiores facti
sunt, legatos ad eum mittunt nobilissimos civitatis, cuius
legationis Nammeius et Verucloetius principem locum ob-
10 tinebant, qui dicerent sibi esse in animo sine ullo maleficio
iter per provinciam facere, propterea quod aliud iter habe-
rent nullum: rogare ut eius voluntate id sibi facere liceat.
Caesar, quod memoria tenebat L. Cassium consulem occisum exercitumque eius ab Helvetiis pulsum et sub iugum
15 missum, concedendum non putabat; neque homines inimico
animo, data facultate per provinciam itineris faciendi, tem-
peraturos ab iniuria et maleficio existimabat. Tamen, ut
spatium intercedere posset dum milites quos imperaverat
convenirent, legatis respondit diem se ad deliberandum
20 sumpturum: si quid vellent, ad Id. April. reverterentur.

COMMENTARY, 1.1–7

Book 1. Chapters 1–7: A description of Gaul and the intended migration of the Helvetii into Roman territory. The year is 58.

1. **Gallia est omnis divisa in partis tris:** One of the best known of Caesar's sayings. Its only likely rivals are *alea iacta est,* "the die is cast," spoken before his crossing the river Rubicon in January 49, the act which initiated civil war; *veni, vidi, vici* (a fine tricolon with alliteration), his communication to the Senate after the Battle of Zela in 47; and *et tu, Brute,* to Brutus as the latter stabbed him on the fateful Ides of March 44. (But Suetonius reports that Caesar spoke his last words to Brutus in Greek—"You too, my son"—and many believed that Brutus was Caesar's illegitimate son.) When the historian Tacitus began his essay on the Germans, the *Germania,* in the year A.D. 98, his first two words were *Germania omnis,* evoking Caesar.

   lingua, institutis, legibus: Another tricolon, well-balanced with words of two syllables, four syllables, and three syllables, with alliteration of the first and last.

   Garumna, Matrona, Sequana: The rivers Garonne in southwest Gaul, north of the Pyrenees, and the Marne and Seine in the northeast.

   dividit: The verb is singular rather than plural, because *Matrona* and *Sequana* together make a single border and are therefore one concept. When there are several subject words which are separated, the verb may agree with the nearest one or ones.

   cultu atque humanitate: The words describe the civilization and quality of life in the advanced Roman empire. Their absence is often taken as a mark of primitive societies.

   provinciae: The extreme southern part of Gaul, known as Gallia Narbonensis, it was established as a Roman province in 121; its prime purpose perhaps was to link Italy with the provinces of Spain. Its chief city was Massilia (Marseille), which had been founded by the Greeks centuries before. It is the modern Provence.

mercatores: Trade was an important means of spreading Roman culture, by introducing products previously unknown to the tribes whom they visited, such as wine, by the use of coinage, and by importing to Rome novelties like amber. Traders reached as far to the north as Scandinavia.

ad effeminandos animos: A gerundive of purpose.

Rhenum: The Rhine.

continenter bellum gerunt: A significant contrast with the meaning of the gerundive above. Warriors are anything but effeminate, and Caesar gives a hint how fierce his future opponents will be.

Helvetii: Their home was in what is now Switzerland. The sentence is transitional, because it links them and the Belgae closely. Both tribes have constant struggles with the Germans; thus Caesar's future enemies are clearly distinguished.

Eorum: The remainder of this paragraph is in some respects suspect. Its style seems un-Caesarean and insufficiently clear. Does *eorum* refer to the Gauls or to the Germans? If the latter, which seems more logical, it follows hard upon the same word in the previous clause. If the former, it gains nothing to say that Gauls occupy Gallic territory. Because the texts of ancient authors depend upon manuscripts which have generally survived by chance, such that some authors may survive in only one while others may occur in many more, it is the editor's task to produce a text which makes sense and fits, as well as possible, the author's style and other characteristics.

ab Sequanis et Helvetiis: A very peculiar construction. Does it mean "From the territory of"? This seems unlikely; perhaps "In the direction of."

ad inferiorem partem: The lower course of the Rhine, that is, the northern part, leading to the North Sea.

spectant . . . orientem solem: The land of the Galli faces essentially north, that of the Belgae north and east, that of the Aquitani west and north.

septentriones: These stars are those clustered near the North Pole which make up the Great and Little Bears.

2. **Orgetorix:** A Celtic name meaning "King of Assassins." His superiority over other Helvetians by birth and wealth clearly played

a role in his outstanding *auctoritas.* He appears in no other source of the history of these times.

M. Messala et M. Pupio Pisone consulibus: Use of an ablative absolute with the names of the year's consuls is a regular means of indicating years in historical contexts. This pair was in office in 61.

coniurationem nobilitatis: Caesar may have wished his readers to recall the conspiracy of Catiline of two years before in Rome.

perfacile esse: Implied indirect discourse, depending upon an understood verb such as *dicens* or the verb *persuasit,* which seems to be too far away to have come readily to mind.

undique loci natura Helvetii continentur: The desire to gain more territory for one's own people has been one of the major causes of migrations and wars over millennia. In the twentieth century, the need for *Lebensraum* was one of the main excuses for German aggressions under the Nazis.

una . . . altera . . . tertia: Caesar had used this expression in the first sentence of the first chapter, with *aliam* in lieu of *altera.*

lacu Lemanno: Lake Geneva.

His rebus fiebat: "Because of these circumstances it happened."

pro: Among the meanings of *pro* is "considering."

milia passuum: *Mille passuum* is the equivalent of the English mile, being approximately nine-tenths of the latter.

3. **constituerunt:** The subject is the *Helvetii.*

pertinerent: Caesar uses the subjunctive here because he is reporting the thoughts of the Helvetians rather than his own. The expression *(ea) quae ad aliquid . . . pertinere* means, among other possibilities, "be relevant (to)" or "be needed (for)."

sementis: *sementis, -is,* f. "to grow as many crops as possible."

in tertium annum: This meant that they would begin their migration in the year 59, which, as it turned out, was the year of Caesar's first consulship. He was to be assigned the province of Gallia Cisalpina, a province in northern Italy on the other side of the Alps from the Helvetii. Their actions would clearly concern him as consul and later as proconsul.

lege: This was not a *lex* in the Roman sense but rather an agreement among the nobility and leading warriors of the tribe, with approval by the tribe as a whole in assembly.

obtinuerat: "Held" rather than "obtained."

populi Romani amicus: An honorary title granted by the Senate to leading men of "barbarian" tribes, as a first step to winning their favor and allegiance, both to gain support if needed in warfare and to guarantee neutrality in appropriate circumstances.

Dumnorigi: Dative with *persuadet,* a few lines below.

filiam suam in matrimonium dat: Orgetorix's plans all along clearly aimed at his gaining the kingship over his people. The Sequani and the Aedui were the tribes immediately west of Helvetia, the latter beyond the former, and he desired kings with whom to treat among those peoples. The most effective means of alliance was marriage to a close relative of a potential ally, ideally a daughter or sister, who then would draw support from the nobility of her native tribe and serve as a kind of hostage to guarantee peaceful relations.

factu: Ablative supine.

obtenturus esset: Since there is no future subjunctive form, the future active participle is often used with a form of *esse* to express futurity.

quin: Clauses introduced by *quin* follow expressions of doubt: *non dubito quin* means "I do not doubt but that."

plurimum possent: "Would be the most powerful."

fidem et ius iurandum: The former word refers to a relationship among the three men, the latter to an oath which they take to abide by this close relationship. The words are an example of hendiadys.

totius Galliae potiri: *Potior* governs the genitive when it means "to become master of."

4.   **per indicium:** "By information from an informer."

Moribus suis: The subject to which the reflexive refers is, of course, the Helvetii.

causam dicere: "To plead his case."

damnatum: This is the object of *sequi,* and has a conditional sense, "if condemned." Caesar may well have wished to place the words *damnatum* and *poenam* together for emphasis.

oportebat: The verb *oportet* governs either a subjunctive without *ut* or an infinitive.

Die constituta causae dictionis: An example of both chiasmus and alliteration. *Causae* is an objective genitive with *dictionis.* Each pair of words is of the same length, the shorter two syllables, the longer four.

familiam: Not "family," but "slaves."

clientis: His retinue.

obaeratos: "Those who were in debt to him."

eodem: A directional adverb, not a pronoun.

ne causam diceret: A negative purpose clause.

Cum . . . conaretur . . . cogerent: A clause of attendant circumstance. The use of the subjunctive in the subordinate clause explains the circumstances under which the action of the main clause takes place. After the lengthy subordinate clauses, the brevity of the main clause is almost anticlimactic.

ipse sibi mortem consciverit: "He committed suicide." The verb is the perfect of *conscisco.*

5. **ut domum:** This is a carefully wrought long clause. The ablative absolute consists of four words, *domum reditionis spe sublata*, as does the gerundive of purpose, *ad omnia pericula subeunda*, with the adjective *paratiores* between them. The accusative *domum* depends upon the implied verb of motion in *reditionis.*

    molita cibaria: "Ground meal."

    Rauricis et Tulingis et Latovicis: The Raurici are to the north of the Helvetii, the Tulingi and Latovici their smaller neighbors. All are located near the Rhine River, in the vicinity of the modern city of Basel.

    cum eis: Because *eis* refers to the Helvetii, one would expect a reflexive, *secum*. But this could cause confusion following closely upon *suis*, referring to the other tribes.

    Boiosque: The Boii were originally a Gallic tribe who had migrated over the centuries to various places before settling in what is now called Bohemia, to the north and east of Italy. They were thus far to the east of Helvetia. Their military prowess was still great. What had begun in Orgetorix's mind as a migration of the Helvetii had now become a far larger movement of peoples. That they should be allowed to pass through Roman territory was unthinkable.

    oppugnarant: Contracted form of *oppugnaverant.*

6. **itinera . . . itineribus:** An unexpected repetition, a practice which
    Caesar occasionally displays. This is an example of a pleonasm.
    qua singuli: Because the route was so narrow, the carts could only
    proceed one at a time, in single file. *Qua* is an adverb, "where."
    perpauci prohibere possent: Alliteration.
    per provinciam nostram: Here at last, as this episode nears its
    end, comes the crucial factor.
    pacati: By the Romans. The Allobroges had been conquered by
    Rome in 121; they revolted in 61 and had been crushed.
    non nullis: Litotes.
    extremum: From the Roman point of view. Geneva lay in the
    north of Helvetia.
    nondum bono animo: This is understandable, as they had only
    recently been reconquered. The ablative is one of description.
    suos . . . eos: The Allobroges and the Helvetii.
    a. d. V. Kal. Apr. L. Pisone, A. Gabinio consulibus: March 28, 58.
    Caesar's consular year was now past and he was proconsul of Cis-
    alpine Gaul, Transalpine Gaul, and Illyricum, the western part of
    what was once Yugoslavia, fronting the Adriatic Sea.

7. **id:** This is explained by the following clause.
    quam maximis . . . itineribus: The distance from Rome to Geneva
    is just under 1000 kilometers, about 620 miles. The most rapid
    march by soldiers recorded is 40 miles (65 km) a day. We may con-
    jecture that Caesar's pace was at least twice that, so that he
    would have arrived in about a week. Plutarch records eight days.
    If Caesar had left Rome in the latter half of March, he would have
    been in the vicinity of Geneva by March 28.
    militum numerum imperat: Caesar responds with characteristic
    speed to the need for more manpower and raises as many as he can.
    legio una: This legion, the famous Tenth, was stationed in the
    province. Caesar deemed it his greatest weapon, for it had served
    under him in Spain in 62 and 61. It remained true to him through
    the civil war. He also had under his command three other le-
    gions, based at Aquileia, a town located at the head of the Adri-
    atic Sea between present-day Venice and Trieste. A legion at full
    strength had 6,000 men. This is a very small number with which
    to plan a defense; thus the levy of troops was crucial.

qui dicerent: A relative clause of purpose, "who should say," "to say."

sibi esse in animo: "It was their intent."

L. Cassium . . . exercitum eius: This had occurred in 107, during the period of the invasions of Roman territories by the Cimbri and Teutones (Germanic tribes) and their allies.

sub iugum missum: After their defeat, the survivors were compelled to "pass under the yoke," made of javelins imbedded into the earth with a horizontal one set across the top. The Romans were compelled to bend low to accomplish this, a sign of submission, which increased the humiliation of the defeated army.

ab iniuria et maleficio: Ablative of separation. The former refers to violence against people, the latter to crimes against their property.

diem: "A certain period of time."

ad Id. April.: April 13. Since the Helvetii began gathering for their great trek on March 28, barely two weeks will have passed. In that brief period, or perhaps slightly longer, word had reached Rome, Caesar had arrived near Geneva, issued his command for further troops, and begun discussions with the Helvetii. The events are remarkably compressed.

LIBER QVARTVS XXIV–XXXVI.I

24. At barbari, consilio Romanorum cognito praemisso equitatu et essedariis, quo plerumque genere in proeliis uti
consuerunt, reliquis copiis subsecuti nostros navibus egredi
prohibebant. Erat ob has causas summa difficultas, quod
5 naves propter magnitudinem nisi in alto constitui non
poterant, militibus autem, ignotis locis, impeditis manibus,
magno et gravi onere armorum oppressis, simul et de
navibus desiliendum et in fluctibus consistendum et cum
hostibus erat pugnandum, cum illi aut ex arido aut paulum
10 in aquam progressi, omnibus membris expeditis, notissimis
locis, audacter tela coicerent et equos insuefactos incitarent.
Quibus rebus nostri perterriti atque huius omnino generis
pugnae imperiti, non eadem alacritate ac studio quo in
pedestribus uti proeliis consuerant utebantur.

25. Quod ubi Caesar animadvertit, navis longas, quarum et
species erat barbaris inusitatior et motus ad usum expe-
ditior, paulum removeri ab onerariis navibus et remis
incitari et ad latus apertum hostium constitui atque inde
5 fundis, sagittis, tormentis hostis propelli ac summoveri
iussit; quae res magno usui nostris fuit. Nam et navium
figura et remorum motu et inusitato genere tormentorum
permoti barbari constiterunt ac paulum modo pedem ret-
tulerunt. Atque nostris militibus cunctantibus, maxime
10 propter altitudinem maris, qui decimae legionis aquilam
ferebat, contestatus deos, ut ea res legioni feliciter eveniret,
'Desilite,' inquit, 'milites, nisi vultis aquilam hostibus
prodere ego certe meum rei publicae atque imperatori
officium praestitero.' Hoc cum voce magna dixisset, se ex
15 navi proiecit atque in hostis aquilam ferre coepit. Tum nostri
cohortati inter se, ne tantum dedecus admitteretur, universi

ex navi desiluerunt. Hos item ex †proximis primis† navibus
cum conspexissent, subsecuti hostibus appropinquarunt.

26.   Pugnatum est ab utrisque acriter. Nostri tamen, quod
neque ordines servare neque firmiter insistere neque
signa subsequi poterant atque alius alia ex navi quibus-
cumque signis occurrerat se aggregabat, magnopere per-
turbabantur; hostes vero, notis omnibus vadis, ubi ex 5
litore aliquos singularis ex navi egredientis conspexerant,
incitatis equis impeditos adoriebantur, plures paucos circum-
sistebant, alii ab latere aperto in universos tela coicie-
bant. Quod cum animadvertisset Caesar, scaphas longarum
navium, item speculatoria navigia militibus compleri iussit 10
et, quos laborantis conspexerat, his subsidia summittebat.
Nostri, simul in arido constiterunt, suis omnibus consecutis,
in hostis impetum fecerunt atque eos in fugam dederunt;
neque longius prosequi potuerunt, quod equites cursum
tenere atque insulam capere non potuerant. Hoc unum 15
ad pristinam fortunam Caesari defuit.

27.   Hostes proelio superati, simul atque se ex fuga receperunt,
statim ad Caesarem legatos de pace miserunt; obsides
daturos quaeque imperasset sese facturos polliciti sunt.
Una cum his legatis Commius Atrebas venit, quem supra
demonstraveram a Caesare in Britanniam praemissum. 5
Hunc illi e navi egressum, cum ad eos oratoris modo
Caesaris mandata deferret, comprehenderant atque in vin-
cula coiecerant: tum proelio facto remiserunt. In petenda
pace eius rei culpam in multitudinem coiecerunt et propter
imprudentiam ut ignosceretur petiverunt. Caesar questus 10
quod, cum ultro in continentem legatis missis pacem ab
se petissent, bellum sine causa intulissent, ignoscere im-
prudentiae dixit obsidesque imperavit; quorum illi partem
statim dederunt, partem ex longinquioribus locis accersitam
paucis diebus sese daturos dixerunt. Interea suos remi- 15

grare in agros iusserunt, principesque undique convenire
et se civitatesque suas Caesari commendare coeperunt.

28.   His rebus pace confirmata, post diem quartum quam
       est in Britanniam ventum naves xviii, de quibus supra
       demonstratum est, quae equites sustulerant, ex superiore
       portu leni vento solverunt. Quae cum appropinquarent
     5 Britanniae et ex castris viderentur, tanta tempestas subito
       coorta est ut nulla earum cursum tenere posset, sed aliae
       eodem unde erant profectae referrentur, aliae ad inferiorem
       partem insulae, quae est propius solis occasum, magno sui
       cum periculo deicerentur; quae tamen, ancoris iactis, cum
    10 fluctibus complerentur, necessario adversa nocte in altum
       provectae, continentem petierunt.

29.   Eadem nocte accidit ut esset luna plena, qui dies mari-
       timos aestus maximos in Oceano efficere consuevit, nos-
       trisque id erat incognitum. Ita uno tempore et longas
       navis, quibus Caesar exercitum transportandum curaverat
     5 quasque in aridum subduxerat, aestus compleverat et
       onerarias, quae ad ancoras erant deligatae, tempestas ad-
       flictabat, neque ulla nostris facultas aut administrandi aut
       auxiliandi dabatur. Compluribus navibus fractis, reliquae
       cum essent funibus, ancoris, reliquisque armamentis amissis
    10 ad navigandum inutiles, magna, id quod necesse erat
       accidere, totius exercitus perturbatio facta est. Neque
       enim naves erant aliae quibus reportari possent, et omnia
       deerant quae ad reficiendas navis erant usui et, quod
       omnibus constabat hiemare in Gallia oportere, frumentum
    15 his in locis in hiemem provisum non erat.

30.   Quibus rebus cognitis, principes Britanniae, qui post
       proelium ad Caesarem convenerant, inter se collocuti, cum
       equites et navis et frumentum Romanis deesse intellegerent

et paucitatem militum ex castrorum exiguitate cognoscerent,
quae hoc erant etiam angustiora quod sine impedimentis 5
Caesar legiones transportaverat, optimum factu esse duxerunt, rebellione facta, frumento commeatuque nostros prohibere et rem in hiemem producere, quod eis superatis aut
reditu interclusis neminem postea belli inferendi causa in
Britanniam transiturum confidebant. Itaque, rursus co- 10
niuratione facta, paulatim ex castris discedere ac suos clam
ex agris deducere coeperunt.

31.   At Caesar, etsi nondum eorum consilia cognoverat, tamen
et ex eventu navium suarum et ex eo quod obsides dare
intermiserant fore id quod accidit suspicabatur. Itaque
ad omnis casus subsidia comparabat. Nam et frumentum
ex agris cotidie in castra conferebat et, quae gravissime 5
adflictae erant naves, earum materia atque aere ad reliquas
reficiendas utebatur et quae ad eas res erant usui ex con-
tinenti comportari iubebat. Itaque, cum summo studio
a militibus administraretur, xii navibus amissis, reliquis ut
navigari commode posset effecit.   10

32.   Dum ea geruntur, legione ex consuetudine una frumentatum missa quae appellabatur septima, neque ulla ad id
tempus belli suspicione interposita, cum pars hominum in
agris remaneret, pars etiam in castra ventitaret, ei qui pro
portis castrorum in statione erant Caesari nuntiaverunt 5
pulverem maiorem quam consuetudo ferret in ea parte
videri quam in partem legio iter fecisset. Caesar id quod
erat suspicatus, aliquid novi a barbaris initum consili,
cohortis quae in stationibus erant secum in eam partem
proficisci, ex reliquis duas in stationem cohortis succedere, 10
reliquas armari et confestim sese subsequi iussit. Cum
paulo longius a castris processisset, suos ab hostibus premi
atque aegre sustinere et conferta legione ex omnibus partibus tela coici animadvertit. Nam quod omni ex reliquis
partibus demesso frumento pars una erat reliqua, suspicati 15

hostes huc nostros esse venturos noctu in silvis delituerant;
tum dispersos, depositis armis in metendo occupatos subito
adorti, paucis interfectis reliquos incertis ordinibus pertur-
baverant, simul equitatu atque essedis circumdederant.

33. Genus hoc est ex essedis pugnae. Primo per omnis partis
perequitant et tela coiciunt atque ipso terrore equorum et
strepitu rotarum ordines plerumque perturbant et, cum se
inter equitum turmas insinuaverunt, ex essedis desiliunt et
5 pedibus proeliantur. Aurigae interim paulatim ex proelio
excedunt atque ita currus collocant ut, si illi a multitudine
hostium premantur, expeditum ad suos receptum habeant.
Ita mobilitatem equitum, stabilitatem peditum in proeliis
praestant, ac tantum usu cotidiano et exercitatione efficiunt
10 uti in declivi ac praecipiti loco incitatos equos sustinere
et brevi moderari ac flectere et per temonem percurrere et
in iugo insistere et se inde in currus citissime recipere
consuerint.

34. Quibus rebus perturbatis nostris novitate pugnae tempore
opportunissimo Caesar auxilium tulit: namque eius adventu
hostes constiterunt, nostri se ex timore receperunt. Quo
facto, ad lacessendum et ad committendum proelium alie-
5 num esse tempus arbitratus suo se loco continuit et, brevi
tempore intermisso, in castra legiones reduxit. Dum haec
geruntur, nostris omnibus occupatis, qui erant in agris
reliqui discesserunt. Secutae sunt continuos compluris
dies tempestates quae et nostros in castris continerent et
10 hostem a pugna prohiberent. Interim barbari nuntios in
omnis partis dimiserunt paucitatemque nostrorum militum
suis praedicaverunt et quanta praedae faciendae atque in
perpetuum sui liberandi facultas daretur, si Romanos castris
expulissent, demonstraverunt. His rebus celeriter magna
15 multitudine peditatus equitatusque coacta ad castra venerunt.

35.   Caesar etsi idem quod superioribus diebus acciderat
fore videbat, ut, si essent hostes pulsi, celeritate periculum
effugerent, tamen nactus equites circiter xxx, quos Commius
Atrebas, de quo ante dictum est, secum transportaverat,
legiones in acie pro castris constituit. Commisso proelio, 5
diutius nostrorum militum impetum hostes ferre non potuerunt ac terga verterunt. Quos tanto spatio secuti
quantum cursu et viribus efficere potuerunt, compluris ex
eis occiderunt, deinde omnibus longe lateque aedificiis
incensis se in castra receperunt.   10

36.   Eodem die legati ab hostibus missi ad Caesarem de pace
venerunt.

COMMENTARY TO 4.24–36.1

Book 4. Chapters 24–36.1: Caesar plans to invade Britain. The results of this campaign. The year is 55.

Book 4 is divided almost equally between the campaign against the Germans and that against the Britons. The former is narrated in chapters 1–19, the latter in chapters 20–36, with the remaining two concerned with affairs in Gaul when the Romans returned from Britain. Planning for the invasion begins in chapter 20. We do not know from what port he sailed, but Portus Itius (Boulogne) seems the most likely, with the planned landing at Dover.

24. **essedariis:** An *essedum* was a light war chariot, a valuable weapon against infantry because of its speed and maneuverability. Contrary to the widespread belief promulgated in books, movies, and television offerings, these chariots did not have razor-sharp blades attached to their wheels.

prohibebant: The last of four words beginning with the letter *p, praemisso, plerumque, proeliis* preceding it. This alliteration tends to hold the long sentence together.

militibus: Dative of agent, depending upon *desiliendum.*

locis . . . impeditis . . . oppressis: A tricolon, with varying constructions.

membris expeditis: This ablative responds to the Romans' *impeditis manibus, notissimis locis* to *ignotis locis,* and the final clause to that which concludes the narration of the Romans' woes.

generis: Objective genitive.

alacritate ac studio: Depend upon *utebantur.*

25. **navis longas:** These were the prime "battleships" of the Roman navy, although at this time there was no standing navy, as it were. Ships were built or requisitioned for specific purposes. Another name for this ship is "trireme," where the emphasis is upon the means of propulsion. These ships were approximately 150 feet (46 m) long. Obviously Caesar was correct in his judgment how the sight of these ships would affect the Britons.

onerariis navibus: Supply ships.

ad latus apertum: The ships were moved some distance so that the soldiers then faced the enemy flank, which was undefended.

fundis, sagittis, tormentis: A tricolon. The *funda* was a sling, which could hurl lead pellets substantial distances. The *tormentum* was an artillery piece, likely a catapult, which we may assume was also unknown to the enemy.

usui: Dative of purpose.

qui: "He who," the legionary standard bearer, the *aquilifer*. It was a disgrace for every soldier if the legionary standard, an eagle of silver or bronze mounted on a staff, was lost to the enemy. As is so often the case in battle, one man made the difference.

Scale model of a catapult. Museo della Civiltà Romana, Rome. (Photograph by H. W. Benario)

proximis primis: These two words, as shown by the use of the obeli, must have been corrupted in the long history of the manuscript tradition. The simple emendation to *primi* makes good sense.

26. **alius alia ex navi:** "Someone from another ship."
    hostes vero: Caesar has neatly balanced the construction of this long sentence. The beginning of each clause is similar, *Nostri tamen . . . hostes vero*, and there are several verbs in each. The Romans are presented in increasing number, *singulares*, "one by one," then *paucos*, finally *in universos*. The entire battle would have covered a half-mile (.8 km) or more.
    ab latere aperto: The Britons threw their weapons from the Romans' right, since the latter were unprotected from that side; the right hand carried the *gladius*, the left arm bore the *scutum*.
    scaphas: Small, light boats, "skiffs."
    speculatoria navigia: "Spy-boats." Both boats were fast and maneuverable. How many men each could carry is unknown.
    suis omnibus consecutis: "Having caught up with their own units."
    neque: Has an adversative as well as a negative sense, "but not."
    capere: Not "capture," but "reach." The ships bearing the cavalry faced headwinds and had to turn back.
    pristinam fortunam: "His former (usual) good fortune."

27. **Commius:** The Atrebates were a tribe who lived in Belgae territory near the English Channel. Caesar showed his regard for Commius early in his preparation for the present campaign. When, earlier in the year, numerous tribes sent embassies to Caesar and promised submission, he accepted these offers and sent the ambassadors home. Commius accompanied them, *quem ipse Atrebatibus superatis regem ibi constituerat, cuius et virtutem et consilium probabat et quem sibi fidelem esse arbitrabatur cuiusque auctoritas in his regionibus magni habebatur, mittit* (4.21). ("He sends Commius, whom he himself [Caesar], after the defeat of the Atrebates, had appointed king there, whose excellence and counsel he continually tested and whom he thought faithful to him and whose influence in these regions [Britain] was considered great.")

Use of the word *auctoritas* evokes Commius' prestige. It does not mean "authority," which refers to the power inherent in a position, such as *imperium* or *potestas*, but rather a quality of influence and respect which an individual possessed. The passage comes from chapter 21.

oratoris: Not "orator," but "envoy" or "representative."

questus: From *queror*.

suos: The object of *iusserunt*, not adjective with *agros*.

principesque: The importance of this clause, which describes the complete submission of a tribe by the appearance before Caesar of all their leading men, is underscored by the extensive alliteration, *convenire, civitatesque, Caesari, commendare, coeperunt*. The previous sentence had also concluded with alliteration, *diebus, daturos, dixerunt*.

28.   **post diem quartam:** The ships approached on the fourth day: Roman numerical measurement was inclusive of the first day and the last. We would likely say "on the third day after our arrival."

    ex superiore portu: "From the harbor to the north," as the coast of Gaul at this point runs essentially in a north–south line.

    ex castris: Caesar's camp is generally placed in the vicinity of present-day Walmer, northeast of Dover and just south of Deal.

    ad inferiorem partem insulae, quae est propius solis occasum: "To the more southern part, which is further west."

    deicerentur: "They were driven."

29.   **ut esset luna plena:** The clause, one of result, is the subject of *accidit*.

    incognitum: This seems odd, as the ships which Caesar used, and their crews, were Gallic. The captains must surely have known the pattern of the sea.

    longas naves: In chapter 24 Caesar remarks that these ships were too large to be grounded in shallow water. The Latin text of this sentence causes considerable difficulty and has evoked numerous emendations.

    administrandi aut auxiliandi: The two verbs mean essentially the same thing. The genitive is objective.

magna: The word gains emphasis by preceding its noun, *pertur-batio*, by a substantial distance.

id quod: Refers to *magna*.

necesse erat: Not "necessary," but "was bound."

Neque enim: This was indeed a crisis, with no other ships available, no obvious means of repairing those which were damaged, no provisions available, and the summer season nearing its end.

30. **sine impedimentis:** All the support material of an army on the march, including pack animals and heavy equipment, had been left in Gaul, with the obvious intent of having it brought once their landing had been consolidated.

   factu: Supine.

   rebellione: "Renewal of war" rather than "rebellion."

   producere: "To extend," "to drag out."

   rursus: "Once again."

   paulatim . . . clam: These adverbs give emphasis to the word *coniuratione*; things were done gradually and in secret.

31. **ex eo:** "From the fact that."

   subsidia comparabat: "Made provision."

   usui: Dative of purpose.

   amissis, reliquis: The collocation of these two words is emphatic. There were about eighty transport ships when the invasion began (see 22.3). The repairs enabled sixty-eight to function and return to Gaul.

   effecit: Caesar's name appears at the very beginning of the chapter, this verb at the very end. The entire subject matter hinges upon him.

32. **ex consuetudine:** This is construed with *una*, rather than *missa*. Its position is crucial.

   frumentatum: Supine.

   in castra ventitaret: This seems rather odd from the Roman point of view, as the Britons were thereby enabled to gain closer information about the size of the Roman army and the state of their supplies and weaponry.

id quod erat: "That which was the case."

novi . . . consilii: Partitive genitive.

in stationibus: There were four gates, each with a cohort on guard. Now a half-cohort succeeded on duty.

cohortis . . . iussit: This is a straightforward yet complex construction. There are three accusative-infinitive pairs, beginning with *cohortis*, continuing with *duas*, concluding with *reliquas*. One can almost follow Caesar's thoughts as he deploys his troops.

conferta: From *confercio*.

demesso: From *demeto*, "harvested."

delituerant: From *delitesco*, "had concealed themselves."

incertis ordinibus: The normal fighting ranks could not be established.

33. **essedis:** Fighting from chariots was characteristic of both Gauls and Britons (see 24). Two men were on a chariot, the warrior and the driver. The most illustrious chariot warrior in Romano-British history was the brilliant queen Boudica, who led a violent revolt against Rome in the year A.D. 60 and destroyed three cities, until finally defeated in battle, after which she committed suicide.

terrore equorum et strepitu rotarum: An example of synchysis.

inter equitum turmas: In this battle, however, the Romans had no cavalry. The aim was to maim or kill the horses.

illi . . . ad quos: The former are the warriors, the latter the drivers.

mobilitatem equitum, stabilitatem peditum: Again synchysis.

peditum in proeliis praestant: Alliteration.

sustinere: "To maintain control."

temonem . . . in iugo: The *temo* is the pole which connects the yoke, *iugum*, to the chariot.

currus citissime . . . consuerint: Once more alliteration.

consuerint: The subject must be the *Aurigae* mentioned some lines before, but this makes little sense, as they would be unable to maintain proper control over the horses. It must refer to the warriors. This chapter is highly rhetorical.

34. **perturbatis . . . pugnae:** An instance of chiasmus with double alliteration.

nostris: This could be part of an ablative absolute or a dative. The latter seems more likely.

alienum: "Not suitable," "inappropriate."

qui . . . reliqui: The Britons.

faciendae . . . liberandi: Objective genitives.

expulissent: Because the conditional clause is linked with the subjunctive verb of the indirect statement, *expulissent*, which would normally be a future perfect indicative, is attracted to the subjunctive.

35. **nactus:** From *nanciscor*. One may wonder where these cavalry have been, that Caesar only at this stage was able to deploy them. Storms had earlier prevented the arrival of the second fleet carrying the cavalry.

     de quo ante dictum est: See 27.2.

     diutius: "For any length of time."

     impetum: The word is neatly placed between *militum* and *hostes*.

     tanto spatio: An ablative of extent.

     potuerunt . . . occiderunt . . . receperunt: The sentence builds in tension; it is essentially a tricolon.

6.1. **legati . . . missi:** So concludes Caesar's first invasion of Britain. By the end of the chapter the Romans have returned to the continent.

LIBER QVINTVS XXIV–XLVIII

24.   Subductis navibus, concilioque Gallorum Samarobrivae
peracto, quod eo anno frumentum in Gallia propter sicci-
tates angustius provenerat, coactus est aliter ac superioribus
annis exercitum in hibernis collocare, legionesque in pluris
civitates distribuere. Ex quibus unam in Morinos ducendam 5
C. Fabio legato dedit, alteram in Nervios Q. Ciceroni,
tertiam in Esubios L. Roscio; quartam in Remis cum
T. Labieno in confinio Treverorum hiemare iussit. Tris
in †Belgis† collocavit: eis M. Crassum quaestorem et
L. Munatium Plancum et C. Trebonium legatos prae- 10
fecit. Unam legionem, quam proxime trans Padum conscripserat, et cohortis v in Eburones, quorum pars maxima
est inter Mosam ac Rhenum, qui sub imperio Ambiorigis
et Catuvolci erant, misit. Eis militibus Q. Titurium
Sabinum et L. Aurunculeium Cottam legatos praeesse 15
iussit. Ad hunc modum distributis legionibus, facillime
inopiae frumentariae sese mederi posse existimavit. Atque
harum tamen omnium legionum hiberna, praeter eam
quam L. Roscio in pacatissimam et quietissimam partem
ducendam dederat, milibus passuum centum continebantur. 20
Ipse interea, quoad legiones collocatas munitaque hiberna
cognovisset, in Gallia morari constituit.

25.   Erat in Carnutibus summo loco natus Tasgetius, cuius
maiores in sua civitate regnum obtinuerant. Huic Caesar
pro eius virtute atque in se benevolentia, quod in omnibus
bellis singulari eius opera fuerat usus, maiorum locum
restituerat. Tertium iam hunc annum regnantem †inimicis 5
iam multis palam ex civitate et eis auctoribus eum †inter-
fecerunt. Defertur ea res ad Caesarem. Ille veritus, quod
ad pluris pertinebat, ne civitas eorum impulsu deficeret,
L. Plancum cum legione ex Belgio celeriter in Carnutes

43

10 proficisci iubet ibique hiemare, quorumque opera cognoverat Tasgetium interfectum, hos comprehensos ad se
mittere. Interim ab omnibus legatis quaestoribusque
quibus legiones tradiderat certior factus est in hiberna
perventum locumque hibernis esse munitum.

26.   Diebus circiter quindecim quibus in hiberna ventum
est initium repentini tumultus ac defectionis ortum est
ab Ambiorige et Catuvolco; qui, cum ad finis regni sui
Sabino Cottaeque praesto fuissent frumentumque in hiberna
5 comportavissent, Indutiomari Treveri nuntiis impulsi suos
concitaverunt subitoque oppressis lignatoribus magna manu
ad castra oppugnatum venerunt. Cum celeriter nostri arma
cepissent vallumque ascendissent atque una ex parte
Hispanis equitibus emissis equestri proelio superiores fuis-
10 sent, desperata re hostes suos ab oppugnatione reduxerunt.
Tum suo more conclamaverunt, uti aliqui ex nostris ad colloquium prodiret: habere sese quae de re communi dicere
vellent, quibus rebus controversias minui posse sperarent.

27.   Mittitur ad eos colloquendi causa C. Arpineius, eques
Romanus, familiaris Q. Tituri, et Q. Iunius ex Hispania
quidam, qui iam ante missu Caesaris ad Ambiorigem
ventitare consuerat; apud quos Ambiorix ad hunc modum
5 locutus est: sese pro Caesaris in se beneficiis plurimum
ei confiteri debere, quod eius opera stipendio liberatus esset
quod Aduatucis finitimis suis pendere consuesset, quodque
ei et filius et fratris filius ab Caesare remissi essent, quos
Aduatuci obsidum numero missos apud se in servitute
10 et catenis tenuissent; neque id quod fecerit de oppugnatione castrorum aut iudicio aut voluntate sua fecisse
sed coactu civitatis, suaque esse eiusmodi imperia ut non
minus haberet iuris in se multitudo quam ipse in multitudinem. Civitati porro hanc fuisse belli causam, quod
15 repentinae Gallorum coniurationi resistere non potuerit.
Id se facile ex humilitate sua probare posse, quod non adeo

sit imperitus rerum ut suis copiis populum Romanum
superari posse confidat. Sed esse Galliae commune consilium: omnibus hibernis Caesaris oppugnandis hunc esse
dictum diem, ne qua legio alterae legioni subsidio venire 20
posset. Non facile Gallos Gallis negare potuisse, praesertim cum de reciperanda communi libertate consilium
initum videretur. Quibus quoniam pro pietate satisfecerit,
habere nunc se rationem offici pro beneficiis Caesaris:
monere, orare Titurium pro hospitio ut suae ac militum 25
saluti consulat. Magnam manum Germanorum conductam
Rhenum transisse: hanc adfore biduo. Ipsorum esse consilium, velintne prius quam finitimi sentiant eductos ex
hibernis milites aut ad Ciceronem aut ad Labienum
deducere, quorum alter milia passuum circiter quinqua- 30
ginta, alter paulo amplius ab eis absit. Illud se polliceri
et iure iurando confirmare, tutum iter per finis daturum.
Quod cum faciat, et civitati sese consulere, quod hibernis
levetur, et Caesari pro eius meritis gratiam referre. Hac
oratione habita discedit Ambiorix. 35

28.   Arpineius et Iunius quae audierunt ad legatos deferunt.
Illi repentina re perturbati, etsi ab hoste ea dicebantur,
tamen non neglegenda existimabant, maximeque hac re
permovebantur, quod civitatem ignobilem atque humilem
Eburonum sua sponte populo Romano bellum facere ausam 5
vix erat credendum. Itaque ad consilium rem deferunt
magnaque inter eos exsistit controversia. L. Aurunculeius compluresque tribuni militum et primorum ordinum
centuriones nihil temere agendum neque ex hibernis iniussu
Caesaris discedendum existimabant; quantasvis magnas 10
etiam copias Germanorum sustineri posse munitis hibernis
docebant: rem esse testimonio, quod primum hostium impetum multis ultro vulneribus inlatis fortissime sustinuerint;
re frumentaria non premi; interea et ex proximis hibernis
et a Caesare conventura subsidia; postremo quid esset levius 15
aut turpius quam auctore hoste de summis rebus capere
consilium?

29.   Contra ea Titurius sero facturos clamitabat, cum maiores
       manus hostium adiunctis Germanis convenissent aut cum
       aliquid calamitatis in proximis hibernis esset acceptum.
       Brevem consulendi esse occasionem. Caesarem arbitrari
  5   profectum in Italiam; neque aliter Carnutes interficiendi
       Tasgeti consilium fuisse capturos neque Eburones, si ille
       adesset, tanta contemptione nostri ad castra venturos esse.
       Non hostem auctorem sed rem spectare: subesse Rhenum;
       magno esse Germanis dolori Ariovisti mortem et superiores
 10   nostras victorias; ardere Galliam tot contumeliis acceptis
       sub populi Romani imperium redactam, superiore gloria rei
       militaris exstincta. Postremo quis hoc sibi persuaderet, sine
       certa re Ambiorigem ad eiusmodi consilium descendisse?
       Suam sententiam in utramque partem esse tutam: si nihil
 15   esset durius, nullo cum periculo ad proximam legionem per-
       venturos: si Gallia omnis cum Germanis consentiret, unam
       esse in celeritate positam salutem. Cottae quidem atque
       eorum qui dissentirent consilium quem haberet exitum, in
       quo si praesens periculum non, at certe longinqua obsid-
 20   ione fames esset timenda?

30.   Hac in utramque partem disputatione habita, cum a Cotta
       primisque ordinibus acriter resisteretur, 'Vincite,' inquit, 'si
       ita vultis,' Sabinus, et id clariore voce, ut magna pars mili-
       tum exaudiret: 'neque is sum,' inquit, 'qui gravissime ex
  5   vobis mortis periculo terrear: hi sapient; si gravius quid
       acciderit, abs te rationem reposcent qui, si per te liceat,
       perendino die cum proximis hibernis coniuncti communem
       cum reliquis belli casum sustineant, non reiecti et relegati
       longe ab ceteris aut ferro aut fame intereant.'

31.   Consurgitur ex consilio; comprehendunt utrumque et
       orant ne sua dissensione et pertinacia rem in summum
       periculum deducant: facilem esse rem, seu maneant, seu
       proficiscantur, si modo unum omnes sentiant ac probent;
  5   contra in dissensione nullam se salutem perspicere. Res
       disputatione ad mediam noctem perducitur. Tandem dat

Cotta permotus manus: superat sententia Sabini. Pronuntiatur prima luce ituros. Consumitur vigiliis reliqua pars noctis, cum sua quisque miles circumspiceret, quid secum portare posset, quid ex instrumento hibernorum relinquere 10 cogeretur. Omnia excogitantur, quare nec sine periculo maneatur et languore militum et vigiliis periculum augeatur. Prima luce sic ex castris proficiscuntur ut quibus esset persuasum non ab hoste sed ab homine amicissimo Ambiorige consilium datum, longissimo agmine maximisque 15 impedimentis.

32. At hostes, postea quam ex nocturno fremitu vigiliisque de profectione eorum senserunt, collocatis insidiis bipertito in silvis opportuno atque occulto loco a milibus passuum circiter duobus Romanorum adventum exspectabant et, cum se maior pars agminis in magnam convallem de- 5 misisset, ex utraque parte eius vallis subito se ostenderunt, novissimosque premere et primos prohibere ascensu atque iniquissimo nostris loco proelium committere coeperunt.

33. Tum demum Titurius, qui nihil ante providisset, trepidare et concursare cohortisque disponere, haec tamen ipsa timide atque ut eum omnia deficere viderentur; quod plerumque eis accidere consuevit qui in ipso negotio consilium capere coguntur. At Cotta, qui cogitasset haec posse in itinere 5 accidere atque ob eam causam profectionis auctor non fuisset, nulla in re communi saluti deerat et in appellandis cohortandisque militibus imperatoris et in pugna militis officia praestabat. Cum propter longitudinem agminis minus facile omnia per se obire et quid quoque loco faciendum 10 esset providere possent, iusserunt pronuntiare ut impedimenta relinquerent atque in orbem consisterent. Quod consilium etsi in eiusmodi casu reprehendendum non est, tamen incommode accidit: nam et nostris militibus spem minuit et hostis ad pugnam alacriores effecit, quod non sine 15 summo timore et desperatione id factum videbatur. Praeterea accidit, quod fieri necesse erat, ut vulgo milites ab

signis discederent, quae quisque eorum carissima haberet
ab impedimentis petere atque arripere properaret, clamore
20 et fletu omnia complerentur.

34. At barbaris consilium non defuit. Nam duces eorum
tota acie pronuntiare iusserunt, ne quis ab loco discederet,
illorum esse praedam atque illis reservari quaecumque
Romani reliquissent: proinde omnia in victoria posita
5 existimarent. Erant et virtute et †numero pugnandi †pares.
Nostri, tametsi ab duce et a fortuna deserebantur, tamen
omnem spem salutis in virtute ponebant, et quotiens quaeque cohors procurrerat, ab ea parte magnus numerus hostium
cadebat. Qua re animadversa, Ambiorix pronuntiari iubet
10 ut procul tela coiciant neu propius accedant et quam in
partem Romani impetum fecerint cedant: levitate armorum
et cotidiana exercitatione nihil his noceri posse: rursus se
ad signa recipientis insequantur.

35. Quo praecepto ab eis diligentissime observato, cum quaepiam cohors ex orbe excesserat atque impetum fecerat,
hostes velocissime refugiebant. Interim eam partem nudari
necesse erat et ab latere aperto tela recipi. Rursus cum
5 in eum locum unde erant egressi reverti coeperant, et ab
eis qui cesserant et ab eis qui proximi steterant circum-
veniebantur. Sin autem locum tenere vellent, nec virtuti
locus relinquebatur neque ab tanta multitudine coiecta tela
conferti vitare poterant. Tamen tot incommodis conflictati,
10 multis vulneribus acceptis resistebant et magna parte diei
consumpta, cum a prima luce ad horam octavam pugnaretur, nihil quod ipsis esset indignum committebant. Tum
T. Balventio, qui superiore anno primum pilum duxerat,
viro forti et magnae auctoritatis, utrumque femur tragula
15 traicitur; Q. Lucanius eiusdem ordinis, fortissime pugnans,
dum circumvento filio subvenit, interficitur; L. Cotta
legatus omnis cohortis ordinesque adhortans in adversum
os funda vulneratur.

36. His rebus permotus Q. Titurius, cum procul Ambiorigem suos cohortantem conspexisset, interpretem suum
Cn. Pompeium ad eum mittit rogatum ut sibi militi-
busque parcat. Ille appellatus respondit: si velit secum
colloqui, licere; sperare a multitudine impetrari posse, 5
quod ad militum salutem pertineat; ipsi vero nihil nocitum
iri, inque eam rem se suam fidem interponere. Ille cum
Cotta saucio communicat, si videatur, pugna ut excedant
et cum Ambiorige una colloquantur: sperare ab eo de sua
ac militum salute impetrari posse. Cotta se ad armatum 10
hostem iturum negat atque in eo perseverat.

37. Sabinus quos in praesentia tribunos militum circum se
habebat et primorum ordinum centuriones se sequi iubet
et, cum propius Ambiorigem accessisset, iussus arma abicere
imperatum facit suisque ut idem faciant imperat. Interim,
dum de condicionibus inter se agunt longiorque consulto 5
ab Ambiorige instituitur sermo, paulatim circumventus interficitur. Tum vero suo more victoriam conclamant atque
ululatum tollunt impetuque in nostros facto ordines perturbant. Ibi L. Cotta pugnans interficitur cum maxima
parte militum. Reliqui se in castra recipiunt unde erant 10
egressi. Ex quibus L. Petrosidius aquilifer, cum magna
multitudine hostium premeretur, aquilam intra vallum proiecit; ipse pro castris fortissime pugnans occiditur. Illi
aegre ad noctem oppugnationem sustinent: noctu ad unum
omnes desperata salute se ipsi interficiunt. Pauci ex 15
proelio elapsi incertis itineribus per silvas ad T. Labienum legatum in hiberna perveniunt atque eum de rebus
gestis certiorem faciunt.

38. Hac victoria sublatus Ambiorix statim cum equitatu in
Aduatucos, qui erant eius regno finitimi, proficiscitur; neque
noctem neque diem intermittit peditatumque sese subsequi
iubet. Re demonstrata Aduatucisque concitatis, postero
die in Nervios pervenit hortaturque ne sui in perpetuum 5

liberandi atque ulciscendi Romanos pro eis quas acce-
perint iniuriis occasionem dimittant; interfectos esse legatos
duo magnamque partem exercitus interisse demonstrat;
nihil esse negoti subito oppressam legionem quae cum
10 Cicerone hiemet interfici; se ad eam rem profitetur adiu-
torem. Facile hac oratione Nerviis persuadet.

39.   Itaque confestim dimissis nuntiis ad Ceutrones, Grudios,
Levacos, Pleumoxios, Geidumnos, qui omnes sub eorum
imperio sunt, quam maximas manus possunt cogunt et de
improviso ad Ciceronis hiberna advolant, nondum ad eum
5 fama de Tituri morte perlata. Huic quoque accidit, quod
fuit necesse, ut non nulli milites qui lignationis munitionisque causa in silvas discessissent repentino equitum adventu
interciperentur. Eis circumventis, magna manu Eburones,
Nervii, Aduatuci atque horum omnium socii et clientes legio-
10 nem oppugnare incipiunt. Nostri celeriter ad arma concur-
runt, vallum conscendunt. Aegre is dies sustentatur, quod
omnem spem hostes in celeritate ponebant atque hanc adepti
victoriam in perpetuum se fore victores confidebant.

40.   Mittuntur ad Caesarem confestim ab Cicerone litterae,
magnis propositis praemiis, si pertulissent: obsessis omnibus
viis missi intercipiuntur. Noctu ex materia quam muni-
tionis causa comportaverant turres admodum centum xx
5 excitantur incredibili celeritate; quae deesse operi videbantur perficiuntur. Hostes postero die multo maioribus
coactis copiis castra oppugnant, fossam complent. Eadem
ratione, qua pridie, ab nostris resistitur. Hoc idem reliquis
deinceps fit diebus. Nulla pars nocturni temporis ad la-
10 borem intermittitur; non aegris, non vulneratis facultas
quietis datur. Quaecumque ad proximi diei oppugnationem
opus sunt noctu comparantur: multae praeustae sudes,
magnus muralium pilorum numerus instituitur; turres contabulantur, pinnae loricaeque ex cratibus attexuntur. Ipse
15 Cicero, cum tenuissima valetudine esset, ne nocturnum

quidem sibi tempus ad quietem relinquebat, ut ultro militum
concursu ac vocibus sibi parcere cogeretur.

41.   Tunc duces principesque Nerviorum qui aliquem sermonis aditum causamque amicitiae cum Cicerone habebant
colloqui sese velle dicunt. Facta potestate eadem quae
Ambiorix cum Titurio egerat commemorant: omnem esse
in armis Galliam; Germanos Rhenum transisse; Caesaris   5
reliquorumque hiberna oppugnari. Addunt etiam de Sabini
morte; Ambiorigem ostentant fidei faciendae causa. Errare
eos dicunt, si quicquam ab eis praesidi sperent qui suis
rebus diffidant; sese tamen hoc esse in Ciceronem popu-
lumque Romanum animo ut nihil nisi hiberna recusent   10
atque hanc inveterascere consuetudinem nolint: licere illis
incolumibus per se ex hibernis discedere et quascumque
in partis velint sine metu proficisci. Cicero ad haec unum
modo respondit: non esse consuetudinem populi Romani
accipere ab hoste armato condicionem: si ab armis discedere   15
velint, se adiutore utantur legatosque ad Caesarem mittant;
sperare pro eius iustitia quae petierint impetraturos.

42.   Ab hac spe repulsi Nervii vallo pedum ix et fossa pedum
xv hiberna cingunt. Haec et superiorum annorum consuetudine ab nobis cognoverant et quos clam de exercitu habebant captivos ab eis docebantur; sed nulla ferramentorum
copia quae esset ad hunc usum idonea, gladiis caespites   5
circumcidere, manibus sagulisque terram exhaurire videbantur. Qua quidem ex re hominum multitudo cognosci
potuit: nam minus horis tribus milium [p̄. xv] in circui-
tu iii munitionem perfecerunt; reliquisque diebus turris ad
altitudinem valli, falces testudinesque, quas idem captivi   10
docuerant, parare ac facere coeperunt.

43.   Septimo oppugnationis die maximo coorto vento fer-
ventis fusili ex argilla glandis fundis et fervefacta iacula

in casas, quae more Gallico stramentis erant tectae, iacere
coeperunt. Hae celeriter ignem comprehenderunt et venti
5 magnitudine in omnem locum castrorum distulerunt. Hostes
maximo clamore, sicuti parta iam atque explorata victoria,
turris testudinesque agere et scalis vallum ascendere coeperunt. At tanta militum virtus atque ea praesentia animi
fuit ut, cum ubique flamma torrerentur maximaque telorum
10 multitudine premerentur suaque omnia impedimenta atque
omnis fortunas conflagrare intellegerent, non modo demi-
grandi causa de vallo decederet nemo sed paene ne respiceret
quidem quisquam, ac tum omnes acerrime fortissimeque
pugnarent. Hic dies nostris longe gravissimus fuit, sed
15 tamen hunc habuit eventum ut eo die maximus numerus
hostium vulneraretur atque interficeretur, ut se sub ipso
vallo constipaverant recessumque primis ultimi non dabant.
Paulum quidem intermissa flamma et quodam loco turri
adacta et contingente vallum, tertiae cohortis centuriones ex
20 eo quo stabant loco recesserunt suosque omnis removerunt;
nutu vocibusque hostis, si introire vellent, vocare coeperunt:
quorum progredi ausus est nemo. Tum ex omni parte
lapidibus coiectis deturbati, turrisque succensa est.

44.   Erant in ea legione fortissimi viri, centuriones, qui primis
ordinibus appropinquarent, T. Pullo et L. Vorenus. Hi
perpetuas inter se controversias habebant, quinam ante-
ferretur, omnibusque annis de locis summis simultatibus
5 contendebant. Ex his Pullo, cum acerrime ad munitiones
pugnaretur, 'Quid dubitas,'inquit, 'Vorene? aut quem
locum tuae pro laude virtutis spectas? hic dies de nostris
controversiis iudicabit.' Haec cum dixisset, procedit extra
munitiones, quaeque pars hostium confertissima est visa
10 irrumpit. Ne Vorenus quidem sese vallo continet sed
omnium veritus existimationem subsequitur. Tum mediocri
spatio relicto Pullo pilum in hostis immittit, atque unum ex
multitudine procurrentem traicit; quo percusso et exanimato,
hunc scutis protegunt, in hostem tela universi coiciunt
15 neque dant regrediendi facultatem. Transfigitur scutum

Pulloni et verutum in balteo defigitur. Avertit hic casus
vaginam et gladium educere conanti dextram moratur
manum, impeditumque hostes circumsistunt. Succurrit
inimicus illi Vorenus et laboranti subvenit. Ad hunc se
confestim a Pullone omnis multitudo convertit; illum veruto   20
arbitrantur occisum. Gladio comminus rem gerit Vorenus,
atque uno interfecto reliquos paulum propellit: dum cupi-
dius instat, in locum deiectus inferiorem concidit. Huic
rursus circumvento fert subsidium Pullo, atque ambo incolumes compluribus interfectis summa cum laude sese intra   25
munitiones recipiunt. Sic fortuna in contentione et certa-
mine utrumque versavit, ut alter alteri inimicus auxilio
salutique esset neque diiudicari posset, uter utri virtute
anteferendus videretur.

45.   Quanto erat in dies gravior atque asperior oppugnatio, et
maxime quod magna parte militum confecta vulneribus
res ad paucitatem defensorum pervenerat, tanto crebriores
litterae nuntiique ad Caesarem mittebantur; quorum pars
deprehensa in conspectu nostrorum militum cum cruciatu   5
necabatur. Erat unus intus Nervius, nomine Vertico, loco
natus honesto, qui a prima obsidione ad Ciceronem perfu-
gerat, suamque ei fidem praestiterat. Hic servo spe liber-
tatis magnisque persuadet praemiis ut litteras ad Caesarem
deferat. Has ille in iaculo inligatas effert, et Gallus inter   10
Gallos sine ulla suspicione versatus ad Caesarem pervenit. Ab eo de periculis Ciceronis legionisque cogno-
scitur.

46.   Caesar, acceptis litteris hora circiter undecima diei,
statim nuntium in Bellovacos ad M. Crassum quaestorem
mittit, cuius hiberna aberant ab eo milia passuum xxv;
iubet media nocte legionem proficisci celeriterque ad se
venire. Exit cum nuntio Crassus. Alterum ad C. Fabium   5
legatum mittit, ut in Atrebatum finis legionem adducat,
qua sibi iter faciendum sciebat. Scribit Labieno, si rei

publicae commodo facere posset, cum legione ad finis
Nerviorum veniat. Reliquam partem exercitus, quod paulo
10 aberat longius, non putat exspectandam; equites circiter
quadringentos ex proximis hibernis colligit.

47.   Hora circiter tertia ab antecursoribus de Crassi adventu
certior factus, eo die milia passuum xx procedit. Crassum
Samarobrivae praeficit legionemque attribuit, quod ibi impedimenta exercitus, obsides civitatum, litteras publicas,
5 frumentumque omne quod eo tolerandae hiemis causa
devexerat relinquebat. Fabius, ut imperatum erat, non ita
multum moratus in itinere cum legione occurrit. Labienus,
interitu Sabini et caede cohortium cognita, cum omnes ad
eum Treverorum copiae venissent veritus ne, si ex hibernis
10 fugae similem profectionem fecisset, hostium impetum sustinere non posset, praesertim quos recenti victoria efferri
sciret, litteras Caesari remittit: quanto cum periculo legionem ex hibernis educturus esset; rem gestam in Eburonibus
perscribit; docet omnis equitatus peditatusque copias Tre-
15 verorum tria milia passuum longe ab suis castris consedisse.

48.   Caesar, consilio eius probato, etsi opinione trium legionum deiectus ad duas redierat, tamen unum communis
salutis auxilium in celeritate ponebat. Venit magnis itineribus in Nerviorum finis. Ibi ex captivis cognoscit quae
5 apud Ciceronem gerantur quantoque in periculo res sit.
Tum cuidam ex equitibus Gallis magnis praemiis persuadet
uti ad Ciceronem epistolam deferat. Hanc Graecis con-
scriptam litteris mittit, ne intercepta epistola nostra ab
hostibus consilia cognoscantur. Si adire non possit, monet
10 ut tragulam cum epistola ad ammentum deligata intra munitionem castrorum abiciat. In litteris scribit se cum legionibus profectum celeriter adfore; hortatur ut pristinam
virtutem retineat. Gallus periculum veritus, ut erat prae-
ceptum, tragulam mittit. Haec casu ad turrim adhaesit

neque ab nostris biduo animadversa tertio die a quodam 15
milite conspicitur, dempta ad Ciceronem defertur. Ille
perlectam in conventu militum recitat, maximaque omnis
laetitia adficit. Tum fumi incendiorum procul videbantur,
quae res omnem dubitationem adventus legionum expulit.

COMMENTARY, 5.24–48

Book 5. Chapters 24–48: Winter encampments in northern Gaul. Two chieftains raise revolt. The Romans suffer serious defeats and are besieged. Caesar ultimately saves the day. The year is 54.

Book 5 begins with Caesar's second invasion of Britain, which concludes successfuly. This narrative fills the first twenty-three chapters, which are immediately followed by unusual natural difficulties in Gaul, and then by a violent uprising against his army.

24. **concilio:** Caesar held a council each spring with the Gauls, both to test their moods and responsiveness to his orders and to allot the number of cavalry each tribe was to furnish.
Samarobrivae: A town in Gallia Belgica, the modern Amiens.
aliter ac: "In a different way than." The normal routine was for the legions to be quartered together or quite near each other, making enemy attack unlikely.
distribuere: This is the crucial word in the sentence.
Morinos: This tribe occupied territory not far from the Channel, in Belgica.
C. Fabio legato: Gaius Fabius may have been *tribunus plebis* in 55. He served under Caesar from 54 to 49.
Nervios: The Nervii were also in Belgica, to the east of the Morini.
Q. Ciceroni: Quintus Tullius Cicero was the younger brother of the great orator. He was *proconsul* of Asia from 61 to 58, then served under Pompey in the years 57–56, under Caesar from 54 to 52 as *legatus*, and under his brother in 51–50, when Marcus Cicero was governor of Cilicia in southern Asia Minor.
Esubios: The Esubii lived west of the river Sequana (Seine), in Gallia, the largest of the *partes tris* which constituted ancient Gaul.
L. Roscio: Lucius Roscius Fabatus was *tribunus plebis* in 55. He was elected *praetor* for 49, when Caesar was *dictator* for the first time.

Remis: The Remi occupied the southeastern part of Belgica, adjacent to the large territory of the Treveri, located west of the Rhine; modern Luxemburg would have been in the approximate center.

T. Labieno: Titus Labienus was *tribunus plebis* in 63. He was Caesar's chief lieutenant during the entire Gallic War and into the beginning of civil war, from 58 to 49, but then changed sides to serve Pompey.

Belgis: The obeli show that this reading is considered corrupt, because several of the tribes already mentioned lived in the area of Belgica. The generally accepted replacement is *Belgio*, which loosely refers to the northeastern part of Gaul.

M. Crassum: Marcus Licinius Crassus was the son of the Triumvir; he was *quaestor* in 54 and *proquaestor* in the following year.

L. Munatium Plancum: Lucius Munatius Plancus served under Caesar from 54 to 46. He was *proconsul* of Transalpine Gaul after Caesar's death in 44–43 and became *consul* in 42.

C. Trebonium: Gaius Trebonius was *tribunus plebis* in 55 and then served Caesar from 54 to 49. He was elected *consul* for the last three months of the year 45.

Unam legionem: This legion was stationed at Aduatuca, in Belgica, the modern Tongres in The Netherlands.

Padum: The river Po in northern Italy.

conscripserat: This is a new legion which Caesar had enrolled in his province of Gallia Transpadana.

Eburones: The Eburones occupied territory in the extreme northeast of Belgica, between the rivers Meuse and Rhine. Their leading community was Aduatuca.

Ambiorigi et Catuvolci: They were joint kings.

Q. Titurium Sabinum: Quintus Titurius Sabinus was with Caesar probably from the years 58 through 54.

L. Aurunculeium Cottam: Lucius Aurunculeius Cotta served Caesar in the same years as Titurius.

milibus passuum centum: The number must be wrong, for some of the legions were more distant from any of the others.

quoad: Introduces a temporal clause.

cognovisset: The pluperfect subjunctive represents a future perfect verb in a main clause.

25. **Carnutibus:** This tribe lived along the river Liger. Their chief town was Autricum, now Chartres. Their opposition to Rome and Roman supporters may stem from the fact that the chief druids of Gaul had their headquarters among the Carnutes (see 6.13).

se . . . eius: The former is Caesar, the latter Tasgetius.

inimicis . . . interfecerunt: This sentence displays corruption in the manuscript tradition. The generally accepted solution reads *inimici* for the first word and retains *interfecerunt*.

multis palam: This is what particularly concerned Caesar, that there might be many enemies of Rome. The opposition of Tasgetius' enemies was known to all.

quorum . . . hos: The former is dependent upon the latter.

quaestoribus: The quaestorship is the first step in the *cursus honorum* and such a man would be very young.

hiberna . . . hibernis: The word is used in different senses. The former refers to the places chosen for winter quarters, the latter indicates that they have been fortified.

26. **praesto fuissent:** *Praesto* with *esse* often has a negative sense, "to present oneself to someone else in a hostile manner." Here it is quite neutral, meaning "to meet."

Indutiomari: Indutiomarus was introduced at the beginning of this book, in chapters 3 and 4. He was one of the leading men among the Treveri, who had promised Caesar his support and immediately undertook to prepare war.

lignatoribus: "Woodcutters."

oppugnatum: Supine.

una ex parte: One may wonder why Caesar mentions this if there were no other cavalry sent into the field from another part of the camp. Perhaps something like this has disappeared from the text: *ex altera Germanis* (or some other nationality).

parte . . . proelio: The alliterative words, although distant from each other, surround the triple alliteration of *equitibus emissis equestri*.

suo more: The Romans normally negotiated through legates, many barbarians (the Gauls among them) by raising a clamor of approval or dissent.

27. **Mittitur:** The verb is singular even though there are two subjects because they are separated. The singular also emphasizes that Arpineius is the more important person.

C. Arpineius: He is otherwise unknown.

Q. Iunius: The subordinate clause shows that he had frequently been an ambassador on Caesar's behalf. He may well have spoken the native language. The instructive words are *iam ante*, the frequentative *ventitare*, and *consuerat*.

apud quos: "In whose presence." Ambiorix's speech falls into two parts, the first personal, the second public. In the former, he shows his gratitude to Caesar and gives two reasons for it. Then he exempts himself from responsibility for the attack upon the Roman camp.

confiteri: The verb of the indirect statement.

stipendio: "From paying tribute."

in servitute et catenis: This was a violation of the law of nations. Hostages were to be considered "guests" of the people to whom they were sent and treated with the dignity appropriate to their rank. The Aduatuci treated them as slaves.

quod fecerit: Ambiorix claims that he was merely the tool of his people.

suaque esse eiusmodi imperia: This was the norm among the Gauls and Germans with whom the Romans dealt. A king or chieftain could not act without the assent of the tribe's warriors.

Civitati porro: Ambiorix now turns to the most important part of his speech, that which reveals careful planning and plotting.

humilitate: The word suggests a double meaning, his own low position among the Gauls and his inferiority in military strength.

dictum diem: A very shrewd statement on his part.

alterae: A rare alternative for *alteri*.

de reciperanda communi libertate: This clearly was what most Gauls desired, to expel the Romans from their lands and recover their freedom. That the Roman envoys accepted what Ambiorix said at face value does not speak well for them. They fell for all his ploys.

pietate . . . rationem offici: Caesar uses both words to emphasize Ambiorix's treachery. The former word stresses the relationship of man to gods, the latter that of man to man.

pro beneficiis: Caesar emphasizes his actions toward him, repeating the phrase used early in the chapter.

conductam: The Germans had been paid by the Gauls; they were therefore mercenary troops. The words *Magnam manum* would clearly strike terror in the minds of isolated Romans.

Ipsorum: The Roman legates Sabinus and Cotta. Ambiorix now offers a solution to the Romans' dangerous situation, safe conduct to another camp.

28. Caesar's Latin is very straightforward in this chapter. He clearly wished his readers to know what arguments were made in favor of withdrawal.

ab hoste: This is the crucial element, that all information came from the enemy, Ambiorix. The words *auctore hoste* in the last sentence underscore this.

civitatem ignobilem atque humilem: Arpineius and Iunius display great *hubris* in their evaluation of the enemy. It was to cost them dearly.

L. Aurunculeius: This is Cotta. The arguments on this side stem from military men, most of whom were veterans of many campaigns. Emotion plays no role in their reasoning.

rem esse testimonio: "This fact supported that statement"; *testimonio* is a dative of purpose.

ultro: "In addition."

esset: It seems odd that Caesar switched to an indirect question after numerous infinitives in indirect statement. Some manuscripts have *esse*, which may be the preferable reading.

29. **Titurius:** His cognomen was Sabinus, the name which Caesar uses at the beginning of the next chapter.

sero: *Serius* might have been better.

clamitabat: A frequentative verb; "he kept shouting."

convenissent: The subjunctive represents the future perfect indicative.

arbitrari: An accusative subject of the infinitive is missing. Understand *se* or *omnes*.

fuisse capturos: "Would have undertaken."

si ille adesset: Not "if Caesar were present," but "if Caesar were still in Gaul."

nostri: Pronoun, used as an objective genitive.

in utramque partem: "No matter how things turned out" is the sense.

30. **ex vobis:** "Stemming from you." Sabinus makes a powerful point, linking the phrase with *terrear*, with the words *mortis periculo* between them. He subtly charges his opponents with fear of death. It is a rather odd argument, as most of the senior military men oppose him.

    te ... te: The charge becomes personal against Cotta by use of the singular.

    perendino die: "On the day after tomorrow."

    intereant: His warning gains emphasis from the two alliterative pairs at the beginning and end of the clause.

31. **comprehendunt ... orant:** The subjects are the members of the *consilium*, who now seek an agreement after such bitter disagreement on the part of the speakers.

    dissensione: Whatever course they chose to follow, *consensus* was crucial.

    dat ... manus: Cotta finally gives in and surrenders to Sabinus' arguments.

    Sabini: His success here is given prominence by the strong alliteration in *superat sententia Sabini*. The verb *superat* will come to mind in the very near future.

    instrumento hibernorum: After the significant effort involved in stocking a winter camp with food and many other items, very little would now be able to be removed and carried with them.

    homine amicissimo: This description of Ambiorix has been mentioned before. Caesar clearly emphasizes it to underscore Ambiorix's treachery.

    longissimo agmine: A legion of 5,000 to 6,000 men, accompanied by its equipment, artillery pieces, supplies, and pack animals and wagons, could stretch for as much as five miles (8 km) on the march. An enemy could attack one part of the line without another part being aware of what was happening before or behind it. The line of march here was likely Sabinus' legion followed by whatever heavy equipment they had taken, then Cotta's five cohorts, another 2,500 to 3,000 men, with pack animals, if any, following.

32. **At:** The adversative strongly shows that the narrative is going to change, from hope to despair and death for the Romans.

hostes: The word gives the lie to the adjective *amicissimo* of the previous sentence. The reader immediately knows that Sabinus' advice was absolutely wrong.

bipertito: The stationing of troops occurred in two places in the woods, about 2 miles (3 km) apart. Or, perhaps, the meaning is that the ambush was merely 2 miles from the camp.

convallem: The Romans were not only surrounded by the enemy but were also at a much lower elevation than they were. Weapons would fall upon them from above, and they would be unable to assume their regular fighting formations.

premere ... primos prohibere ... proelium: Caesar emphasizes his narrative here by the fourfold alliteration.

33. **trepidare ... concursare ... disponere:** Use of the infinitives gives a vividness to the narrative. Although historical grammatically, the main sense they have here is descriptive.

omnia: All the good qualities of a general, which Titurius Sabinus entirely lacked.

quod ... coguntur: This statement has no role in the narrative but is rather the author's comment (in other words, the commanding general's judgment of a subordinate).

At Cotta: The adversative now introduces in contrast the actions of a fine soldier.

auctor: The word need not refer only to the person responsible for an idea or a plan. It sometimes designates one who supports that which has been proposed.

nulla in re ... praestabat: Caesar gives Cotta the highest praise: he did everything possible for the safety of all, performed both the duties of a commander and those of a soldier.

iusserunt: The sudden switch to the plural expands the action to the other officers under Cotta as well as including him. It appears quite impossible that the plural refers to Sabinus and Cotta. They were widely separated, perhaps by several miles. They could hardly have had any means of communication, and surely Sabinus could not have convinced Cotta to act as he (Sabinus) wished.

in orbem: Roman order of battle was based on ranks and files of men in the formation of a rectangle; base units of some 80 men could be combined into larger rectangles. Here the men are ordered to move from this standard formation into a circle, as they are being attacked from all sides.

34. **pronuntiare:** "to send the word."

virtute ... virtute: Both the Gauls and the Romans possessed *virtus*, but *fortuna* had abandoned the latter.

numero pugnandi: Editors generally consider these words corrupt and remove the sentence. The Romans were outnumbered and, earlier in the work, Caesar claimed that they were braver than Gauls.

eis noceri: Because the verb *noceo* is intransitive, the passive must be expressed by its impersonal use, with the person affected in the dative.

35. **quaepiam:** *Quispiam* is a particular indefinite pronoun, so that the meaning here is "any particular cohort."

nudari: That part of the circle which was thus left empty became the object of assault by the enemy.

nec virtuti locus relinquebatur: When they held their position, they were so closely packed together (*conferti*) that they could not properly handle their weapons. In addition the enemy did not close for hand-to-hand combat.

coiecta ... conferti ... conflictati: The assonance of the three participles, all with disastrous meaning, emphasizes the dire straits of the Romans.

ad horam octavam: The Roman day was divided into twelve parts, beginning with sunup and ending with sundown. Consequently, an hour was much longer in the summer than it was in winter. The longest hour embraced seventy-seven minutes, the shortest forty-three. An hour at this point would have contained about fifty-two minutes, so that the eighth hour would have been about one-thirty in the afternoon.

primum pilum: The centurion in command of a legion.

tragula: A dart hurled like a pellet from a sling.

filio: An interesting human touch.

in adversum os: "Head on in the mouth."

funda: The ammunition of a sling was a small lead pellet, which, hurled at great speed, was much like a modern bullet.

36. **Cn. Pompeium:** This is the only mention of him in the *Bellum Gallicum*. His name will have led many readers to think of Pompey the Great.

    rogatum: Supine.

    velit: The subject is Titurius.

    ipsi: Titurius again.

    nocitum iri: Future passive infinitive.

    Ille: Still Titurius. Caesar places him in the forefront of this humiliating exchange to make clear his responsibility for the disaster.

    sperare: Titurius' hopes and confidence are almost ludicrous, in that he displays at least some trust in Ambiorix.

    impetrari: The verb means "to obtain by seeking," but in this context the sense of "begging" is very strong. It is difficult to imagine the experienced soldier Cotta agreeing to that.

    armatum: Cotta displays his military background; he obviously does not bend toward Ambiorix.

37. **in praesentia:** "For the business at hand."

    imperatum facit: By his actions Sabinus reveals that he has already capitulated and thereby suffers shame of which he seemingly is unaware. Such humiliation disgraces an entire army. It may be compared to "passing under the yoke," the greatest disgrace in Roman military history, as occurred after the Battle of the Caudine Forks against the Samnites in 321.

    consulto: Ambiorix intentionally prolongs discussion, so that his men can prepare for their onslaught.

interficitur: The singular refers, quite obviously, to Sabinus, but by extension embraces those with him.

ululatum: The word suggests, by a kind of onomatopoeia, what the sound is like. It normally refers to mourning and lamentation but here is a cry of celebration.

L. Cotta pugnans: The contrast between Sabinus and Cotta continues until the end. Sabinus dies after capitulation; Cotta fights to the last, doing his duty.

L. Petrosidius aquilifer: The standard bearer, charged with display and protection of the legion's *aquila* (see 4.25), was the most important of what we may call "noncommissioned officers." Loss of an eagle to the enemy was ultimate disgrace for the entire legion. Petrosidius protects that in his charge as best he can, then dies fighting.

noctu ... interficiunt: This must be one of the saddest sentences Caesar ever wrote: "safety comes only with self-inflicted death."

ad T. Labienum: This would have involved enormous danger and physical stamina. Labienus' camp was 50 or more miles (some 80 km) distant, in the territory of the Remi; they escaped without a guide, without food, without any equipment save that which they wore or carried.

Caesar's response to this news is recorded by Suetonius, *Divus Iulius* 67: "He loved his men so much that, after he had heard of Titurius' disaster, he let his beard and hair grow long and did not cut them until he had gotten vengeance." (Translation by J. C. Rolfe) Augustus reacted the same way after Rome's disaster at the hands of the German chieftain Arminius in A.D. 9.

38. **intermittit:** Ambiorix and his cavalry ride without halt, leaving the night after their victory. There must have been a substantial number of additional horses for relief; the usual distance that a horse with rider could cover at speed was about 25 miles (40 km).

ne ... dimittant: The clause is carefully wrought. His arguments and inducements for destroying Roman troops and recovering the freedom of the Gallic tribes precede the object and main verb.

sui . . . liberandi: The forms *sui, sibi, se, se* are both singular and plural. *Sui* here is a plural form, but the more precise construction, *sui . . . liberandorum*, seems quite infelicitous.

nihil . . . negoti: Partitive genitive.

subito oppressam: Ambiorix counts on Cicero's acting in the same way as Sabinus.

39. **quam maximas:** "The very greatest."

nondum . . . perlata: The most significant part of the sentence is delayed until the end, an unaccustomed ablative absolute. Caesar rarely ends a sentence in such a way, but here it emphasizes Cicero's ignorance of Sabinus' disaster and underscores his response to the crisis.

Huic: To Cicero, as it had to Sabinus and Cotta.

quod fuit necesse: Some disaster had to occur so that the commander and his men became aware of the uprising.

non nulli: The words indicate that the number of men was small.

lignationis munitionisque: Hendiadys.

legionem: The contrast with *non nulli* is great.

quod . . . confidebant: This clause is crucial, because it emphasizes the enemy's strategy. Speed is everything, endurance is much less important.

40. This chapter presents the Roman army at its finest when under great pressure. Caesar must have had pleasure, in retrospect, in its writing.

ad Caesarem: Caesar was at Samarobriva, about 175 miles (280 km) distant.

missi intercipiuntur: How the numerous letter carriers ever hoped to get through is a source of wonder, with the roads blocked and riding in enemy territory. The *praemia*, of course, were intended for those *missi*, although *litterae* is much nearer in position.

excitantur: "Raised up, built."

Hostes . . . complent: This is a highly rhetorical sentence, with the synchysis of the ablatives, alliteration of *multo maioribus* and *coactis copiis castra complent*, and the synchysis of the final four words.

ad laborem: "As far as work went."

sudes: These were stakes of substantial size and strength, one end of which was made into a point and hardened in the flame. They were then driven into the ground, facing the enemy.

muralium pilorum: The *pila* were the heavy spears of the infantry. In regular battle, the Roman advance began with the launching of the *pila;* the *gladii* then came into play at close quarters. *Pila* were called *muralia* when hurled from the wall during a siege.

contabulantur: "Raised in height."

pinnae loricaeque: "Pinnacles and parapets."

ultro: "Acting on their own."

41. **duces principesque:** The former are the military commanders, the latter the leading aristocrats of the tribe. Individuals could of course belong to both groups.

sermonis aditum causamque amicitiae: Chiasmus.

Ambiorigem ostentat fidei faciendae causa: This claim would be laughable were it not so serious. The man responsible for the Gallic uprising and an exemplar of treachery is presented as a symbol of truth and integrity.

eos: The Romans.

hanc inveterascere consuetudinem: They do not want winter quarters in their territory, nor do they want this practice to become established.

ab hoste armato: Cf. Cotta's response to Sabinus' proposal to have a meeting with Ambiorix at the end of 36.

pro eius iustitia: This refers to Caesar.

42. **pedum:** With the numeral, a genitive of description.

fossa: The measurement gives the width of the trench. Such military trenches were almost always V-shaped, the depth commensurate with the width.

clam: An interesting comment, because we do not know when they gained these captives. Perhaps it was in the earlier years, when they fought against Caesar.

nulla . . . copia: Is this an ablative absolute, or a nominative without an expressed verb? Probably the former.

ferramentorum: "Iron tools."

Scale model of a battering ram. Museo della Civiltà Romana, Rome.
(Photograph by H. W. Benario)

caespites: "Sections of sod."
manibus sagulisque: "In their hands and cloaks."
[p. XV]: This is clearly a corruption; a circumvallation of 15 miles
(24 km) around one legionary camp is absurd. *III* makes good sense.
falces testudinesque: "Hooks and sheds." The Gauls not only laid
siege to the Roman camp with a wall that matched the Roman
fortification in height, but also prepared tools and weapons with
which they could attack and destroy the enemy's wall.

43. **ferventes fusili ex argilla glandis:** "Heated pellets made of soft-
     ened clay." Note *fervefacta* almost immediately following. The
     four words beginning with the letter *f* begin and end with the
     words referring to heat.
     impedimenta . . . fortunas: The former refers to military equip-
     ment, the latter to their personal belongings.
     se constipaverant: "They had crowded."
     turri adacta et contingente vallum: Chiasmus. The Gauls make
     an attempt to break into the fort.
     deturbati: Who is the subject, Romans or Gauls? In all likelihood,
     the latter.

Model of soldiers at a wall in *testudo* formation. Museo della Civiltà Romana, Rome. (Photograph by H. W. Benario)

44. **qui primis ordinibus appropinquarent:** They were nearing promotion to the position of a cohort's ranking centurion, the *primus pilus*.

habebant: The imperfect shows that their rivalry and mutual dislike had been going on for a long time.

simultatibus: The word indicates how far their dislike for each other extended. *Odium* would have been only a bit stronger.

Ne . . . quidem: Not the customary *not . . . even*, but *certainly . . . not*.

protegunt: The enemy, of course; *universi*, a few words on, makes this clear.

verutum in balteo defigitur: The weapon, whether a dart or, more likely, a javelin, sticks in his swordbelt. Hence the scabbard's position is changed, probably toward his back.

Succurrit inimicus: The collocation of the two words emphasizes the feelings of the two men and, in spite of that, the great
service they do each other. The words *inimicus* and *hostis* have
subtle variations among the acceptable meanings. In essence,
however, the former refers to a personal enemy or an enemy of
the state, the latter to a public enemy, particularly a foreign
people.

ambo . . . interfectis: The synchysis succinctly recapitulates their
escapade, with *ambo* against *compluribus*, the former *incolumes*,
the latter *interfectis*.

45. **Quanto . . . tanto:** These two words are correlatives, *quantus* an
interrogative, *tantus* a demonstrative. The danger increased pro-
portionately to the decreasing number of defenders.

ille in iaculo inligatas: The fourfold alliteration gives emphasis to
the final two words, the fact that the messenger did not carry
any message from Cicero on his person but tied it to his spear.
This interpretation is by no means sure. Some editors prefer to
think that the message was hidden in the spearpoint, which was
hollow and fit over the shaft. But, as seen in chapter 48, that a
message was attached to a spear had to be seen. In the present
instance, it could have been tightly tied to the shaft and covered
with cord.

46. **hora circiter undecima:** The month being October, the time
would be before five in the afternoon.

nuntium: Could this be the same messenger who had brought
Cicero's message to Caesar? In all probability it was a different
man, who, returning to Caesar with Crassus, would have covered
50 miles (80 km) in about sixteen hours.

qua sibi iter faciendum: Caesar knew that he would have to pass
through their territory.

rei publicae commodo: Labienus was encamped near the border of
the Treveri, who presented a significant threat. Therefore Caesar
left it to his judgment whether Labienus could leave his encamp-
ment without inviting a possible Treveran invasion.

47. **Hora circiter tertia:** About nine o'clock in the morning.
milia passuum XX: Twenty miles (32 km) was the usual day's
march of a fully equipped army. Terrain, of course, would make
substantial differences.
litteras publicas: The public records which Caesar, as governor,
was required to keep and which served as source material for his
composition of his *Bellum Gallicum.*
ad eum: "Into his vicinity."
veritus . . . ut: Verbs of fearing are followed by subjunctive clauses,
positive introduced by *ne*, negative by *ut*.
quanto cum periculo: The clause depends upon an understood
verb, drawn from *remittit*, such as *docens*.

48. **Caesar, consilio . . . communis . . . celeritate:** The three alliterative words, although distant from one another, present the common theme of Caesar's strategy. Following soon after Caesar's
name, the word *celeritate* gains emphasis, as the two words bracket
the sentence.
magnis itineribus: The adjective clearly indicates that he covered
more than the normal day's march.
tragulam . . . ammentum: The *tragula*, a Gallic spear, was pro-
pelled by a sling attached to the middle of the shaft, the *ammentum*. It is to this that the letter is attached, and was thereby
visible when the spear was noticed.
retineat: This refers to Cicero, but obviously the sense extends to
the entire garrison.
in conventu: Cicero called a parade of all his men who were able
to attend.
fumi incendiorum: Caesar was burning enemy villages and property as he advanced. He knew that the smoke would be seen by
the besieged.

This last chapter is a virtuoso performance on the part of Caesar.
When he wrote this passage, likely in the winter of 54–53, "peace"
had once more been established, but his narrative rockets along
with a highly emotional impact. The contrast among commanders, Titurius Sabinus on the one hand, Cotta and Quintus Cicero

on the other, is great. The bravery of the Roman soldier, regardless of the odds, is highly praised. A rescue mission is invariably tense, because the fate of many is at stake. One may think of the Battle of Waterloo in 1815, when the arrival of the Prussians in the late afternoon enabled the Duke of Wellington to defeat Napoleon, and to the relief of American paratroopers at Bastogne in December 1944 by General Patton's Third Army.

LIBER SEXTVS XIII–XX

13. In omni Gallia eorum hominum qui aliquo sunt numero atque honore genera sunt duo. Nam plebes paene servorum habetur loco, quae nihil audet per se, nullo adhibetur consilio. Plerique, cum aut aere alieno aut magnitudine tributorum aut iniuria potentiorum premuntur, sese in ser- 5
vitutem dicant nobilibus, *quibus* in hos eadem omnia sunt iura quae dominis in servos. Sed de his duobus generibus alterum est druidum, alterum equitum. Illi rebus divinis intersunt, sacrificia publica ac privata procurant, religiones interpretantur: ad hos magnus adulescentium numerus dis- 10
ciplinae causa concurrit, magnoque hi sunt apud eos honore. Nam fere de omnibus controversiis publicis privatisque con-stituunt et, si quod est admissum facinus, si caedes facta, si de hereditate, de finibus controversia est, idem decernunt, praemia poenasque constituunt; si qui aut privatus aut 15
populus eorum decreto non stetit, sacrificiis interdicunt. Haec poena apud eos est gravissima. Quibus ita est inter-dictum, hi numero impiorum ac sceleratorum habentur, his omnes decedunt, aditum sermonemque defugiunt, ne quid ex contagione incommodi accipiant, neque his petentibus 20
ius redditur, neque honos ullus communicatur. His autem omnibus druidibus praeest unus, qui summam inter eos habet auctoritatem. Hoc mortuo, aut si qui ex reliquis ex-cellit dignitate succedit, aut, si sunt plures pares, suffragio druidum, non numquam etiam armis de principatu con- 25
tendunt. Hi certo anni tempore in finibus Carnutum, quae regio totius Galliae media habetur, considunt in loco consecrato. Huc omnes undique qui controversias habent conveniunt eorumque decretis iudiciisque parent. Disci-plina in Britannia reperta atque inde in Galliam translata 30
esse existimatur, et nunc qui diligentius eam rem cognoscere volunt plerumque illo discendi causa proficiscuntur.

14. Druides a bello abesse consuerunt, neque tributa una cum
reliquis pendunt; militiae vacationem omniumque rerum
habent immunitatem. Tantis excitati praemiis et sua
sponte multi in disciplinam conveniunt et a parentibus
5 propinquisque mittuntur. Magnum ibi numerum versuum
ediscere dicuntur. Itaque annos non nulli xx in disciplina
permanent. Neque fas esse existimant ea litteris mandare,
cum in reliquis fere rebus, publicis privatisque rationibus,
Graecis litteris utantur. Id mihi duabus de causis insti-
10 tuisse videntur, quod neque in vulgum disciplinam efferri
velint neque eos qui discunt litteris confisos minus
memoriae studere; quod fere plerisque accidit ut prae-
sidio litterarum diligentiam in perdiscendo ac memoriam
remittant. In primis hoc volunt persuadere, non interire
15 animas sed ab aliis post mortem transire ad alios, atque
hoc maxime ad virtutem excitari putant, metu mortis
neglecto. Multa praeterea de sideribus atque eorum motu,
de mundi ac terrarum magnitudine, de rerum natura, de
deorum immortalium vi ac potestate disputant et iuventuti
20 tradunt.

15. Alterum genus est equitum. Hi, cum est usus atque
aliquod bellum incidit (quod fere ante Caesaris adventum
quot annis accidere solebat, uti aut ipsi iniurias inferrent
aut inlatas propulsarent), omnes in bello versantur; atque
5 eorum ut quisque est genere copiisque amplissimus, ita
plurimos circum se ambactos clientisque habet. Hanc
unam gratiam potentiamque noverunt.

16. Natio est omnium Gallorum admodum dedita religionibus,
atque ob eam causam qui sunt adfecti gravioribus morbis
quique in proeliis periculisque versantur aut pro victimis
homines immolant aut se immolaturos vovent, administris-
5 que ad ea sacrificia druidibus utuntur; quod, pro vita
hominis nisi hominis vita reddatur, non posse deorum im-

mortalium numen placari arbitrantur, publiceque eiusdem
generis habent instituta sacrificia. Alii immani magnitudine
simulacra habent, quorum contexta viminibus membra vivis
hominibus complent; quibus succensi circumventi flamma   10
exanimantur homines. Supplicia eorum qui in furto aut
in latrocinio aut aliqua noxia sint comprehensi gratiora dis
immortalibus esse arbitrantur, sed, cum eius generis copia
deficit, etiam ad innocentium supplicia descendunt.

17. Deum maxime Mercurium colunt. Huius sunt plurima
simulacra, hunc omnium inventorem artium ferunt, hunc
viarum atque itinerum ducem, hunc ad quaestus pecuniae
mercaturasque habere vim maximam arbitrantur. Post hunc
Apollinem et Martem et Iovem et Minervam. De his   5
eandem fere quam reliquae gentes habent opinionem:
Apollinem morbos depellere, Minervam operum atque
artificiorum initia tradere, Iovem imperium caelestium
tenere, Martem bella regere. Huic, cum proelio dimicare
constituerunt, ea quae bello ceperint plerumque devovent: 10
quae superaverint, animalia capta immolant, reliquasque
res in unum locum conferunt. Multis in civitatibus harum
rerum exstructos tumulos locis consecratis conspicari licet,
neque saepe accidit ut neglecta quispiam religione aut
capta apud se occultare aut posita tollere auderet, gravis-   15
simumque ei rei supplicium cum cruciatu constitutum est.

18.   Galli se omnes ab Dite patre prognatos praedicant, idque
ab Druidibus proditum dicunt. Ob eam causam spatia
omnis temporis non numero dierum sed noctium finiunt;
dies natalis et mensum et annorum initia sic observant
ut noctem dies subsequatur. In reliquis vitae institutis   5
hoc fere ab reliquis differunt quod suos liberos, nisi cum
adoleverunt ut munus militiae sustinere possint, palam ad
se adire non patiuntur filiumque puerili aetate in publico
in conspectu patris adsistere turpe ducunt.

19.   Viri quantas pecunias ab uxoribus dotis nomine accepe-
runt tantas ex suis bonis aestimatione facta cum dotibus
communicant. Huius omnis pecuniae coniunctim ratio
habetur fructusque servantur: uter eorum vita superarit, ad
5 eum pars utriusque cum fructibus superiorum temporum
pervenit. Viri in uxores, sicuti in liberos, vitae necisque
habent potestatem; et cum pater familiae inlustriore loco
natus decessit, eius propinqui conveniunt et, de morte si res
in suspicionem venit, de uxoribus in servilem modum quaes-
10 tionem habent et, si compertum est, igni atque omnibus
tormentis excruciatas interficiunt. Funera sunt pro cultu
Gallorum magnifica et sumptuosa; omniaque quae vivis cordi
fuisse arbitrantur in ignem inferunt, etiam animalia; ac paulo
supra hanc memoriam servi et clientes quos ab eis dilectos
15 esse constabat iustis funeribus confectis una cremabantur.

20.   Quae civitates commodius suam rem publicam adminis-
trare existimantur habent legibus sanctum, si quis quid de
re publica a finitimis rumore aut fama acceperit, uti ad
magistratum deferat neve cum quo alio communicet: quod
5 saepe homines temerarios atque imperitos falsis rumoribus
terreri et ad facinus impelli et de summis rebus consilium
capere cognitum est. Magistratus quae visa sunt occul-
tant, quaeque esse ex usu iudicaverunt multitudini produnt.
De re publica nisi per concilium loqui non conceditur.

COMMENTARY, 6.13-20

Book 6. Chapters 13-20: Warfare against the Nervii and Treveri. Preparations for invading Germany. Discussion of Gallic life, particularly of the druids. Discussion of Germanic life. More warfare. The year is 53.

Book 6 offers a substantial amount of anthropological and ethnological material on the Gauls and Germans. Fighting continues unabated.

13. **sese in servitutem dicant:** This was a practice unknown in Rome. *Servitutem . . . nobilibus : dominis . . . servos* forms a powerful chiasmus.
equitum: "Knights," not "cavalry." This is clear from the previous words *aliquo . . . honore.*
praemia poenasque: This seems to be linked only with *si caedes facta,* mentioned a little before. *Praemia* must refer to the financial compensation which the deceased's survivors receive, *poenas* to the punishments imposed upon the killer.
interdicunt: "Forbid participation, excommunicate."
his . . . decedunt: "They get out of their way," in order not to meet them.
Carnutum: The Carnutes lived along the river Liger (Loire), near Orléans; their main city (Autricum) is now Chartres.
Britannia: This was indeed true, and druidism would survive there longer than in Gaul, where the Romans undertook to suppress the religion and extirpate the priests, in order to end their appalling use of human sacrifice and to destroy their moral and political influence.
Caesar and Tacitus, who wrote more than a century and a half later, are our prime sources about the druids. The druids and their supporters were bitter fighters and enemies. Tacitus wrote of the invasion of the island of Mona, now Anglesey, off the northern coast of Wales, to destroy druidism, in 60 A.D. While the army

was occupied there, a terrible uprising began in the east of the island of Britannia, led by the warrior queen Boudica. She won
several great victories and destroyed the cities of Camulodunum
(Colchester), Londinium (London), and Verulamium (St. Albans).
Ultimately she was defeated. The power of the druids was dra-
matically weakened. The relevant sections in Tacitus' *Annales*
are 14.29–39.

14. **annos XX:** This seems quite remarkable, a "basic training" of
twenty years. If a youth came for instruction at age ten, he would
be thirty when he concluded.

Graecis litteris: Surely they knew Latin as well, if they had learned
Greek. But many Gauls and Britons would have learned Latin
from contact with the Romans, particularly from the require-
ments of trade and commerce. The knowledge of Greek among
the Gauls must have stemmed from the south, through Massilia
(Marseille).

mihi: This is the only, the *unique,* instance in the entire work
where Caesar refers to himself in the first person.

metu mortis neglecto: An ablative absolute concluding a sentence is uncommon in Caesar, but here the emphatic position re-
emphasizes *non interire animas* of a few lines earlier.

Multa praeterea: This long sentence concludes the druid section
by focusing upon their scientific and philosophical studies. Lu-
cretius' great poem *De rerum natura* had been published about
a year before Caesar wrote this book; is he hinting that he was
familiar with it?

15. **equitum:** Early in chapter 13 Caesar had written, *Sed de his duobus generibus alterum est druidum, alterum equitum.*

usus: "Need."

copiisque . . . plurimos . . . clientisque: A man of rank and prestige would have many followers. The greater the number, the
greater his distinction. Tacitus reports the same in his *Germania*
(13–14), written in A.D. 98.

ambactos: This is a word of Celtic origin which the Romans ad-
opted. It means "vassal" or "dependent," not a slave nor a client.

16. **religionibus:** "Superstitions."
in proeliis periculisque: An instance of hendiadys, "in the dangers of battles," emphasized by the alliteration of the initial letters.
homines immolant: This was the druid practice which particularly appalled the Romans. It was finally ended in the principates of Augustus and Tiberius.
publiceque . . . sacrificia: There were regular, set occasions when human sacrifice was performed.
viminibus . . . vivis: The two words have a similarly sounding first syllable, but the contrast between an object made of reeds and a human being is great, and frightening.
quibus: Refers to *viminibus.*
furto . . . latrocinio . . . noxia: These words are contrasted with the coming *innocentium.* One may wonder how the priests chose the innocent person or persons for the ceremony.

17. **Mercurium:** Tacitus in his *Germania* (9) devotes only a brief section to the gods of the Germans and their manner of worship. His first sentence copies Caesar: *Deorum maxime Mercurium colunt.* The only other gods whom Tacitus mentions are Hercules and Mars. Both authors describe German religion with Roman names, as Caesar does here in his Gallic context. The chief German god, who was equated by the Romans with Mercury, would in later centuries become known as Wodan.
Huius . . . hunc . . . hunc . . . hunc: Anaphora.
viarum atque itinerum ducem: The former refers to the route of the roads, the latter indicates the guide who helps travelers accomplish their journeys safely.
reliquae gentes: As Caesar is describing the characteristics of the Gallic peoples, one may wonder whom he considers *reliquae gentes.* We know that the Germans are in many regards similar, and Caesar likely thought of them first and foremost.
ceperint: Future perfect, expressing great confidence that they will be victorious.
neglecta . . . religione: This implies that such an individual must be very rare indeed.

gravissimum ... supplicium ... cruciatu: These words give an appropriate somberness to the entire last sentence. The triple alliteration of the letter *c*, with the words increasing in length and significance, adds to the impact.

18. **Dite:** The god *Dis* is linked with Jupiter, but among the Gauls is the god of night and darkness.
    dies natalis: "Birthdays."
    In reliquis vitae institutis: This is a quite remarkable custom, that a parent has no interest in a child until a son reaches the age for military service. Caesar does not indicate what the relationship of a father and daughter is.
    puerili ... publico ... patris: Alliteration. The first and last words are further linked by the family relationship.

19. **dotis:** "Dowry."
    ex suis bonis: Property consists of much more than money: land, animals of various kinds, interest earned on loans.
    coniunctim: "Jointly, in common."
    vita superarit: "Has outlived."
    pars utriusque: "The part of each, the entire sum."
    pater familiae: Perhaps more commonly *paterfamilias.*
    inlustriore loco: It seems odd that the higher rank of the deceased can call forth an inquiry into what occurred and can lead to the torture and death of the wife.
    in servilem modum: "By torture."
    ac paulo supra hanc memoriam: This practice ended before the period of those now living.

20. **consilium capere cognitum:** The alliteration emphasizes the lack of capacity on the part of *homines temerarios atque imperitos* to take sane counsel.
    quaeque: = Ea *quae.*
    produnt: The people learn only good news.

VOCABULARY

An Arabic numeral in parentheses after a verb (1) shows that this is a regular verb of the first conjugation with a sequence of principal parts ending in **-āre, -āvī, -ātum.**

ā *or* **ab,** *prep.* with *abl.*, from, away from; by
abiciō, -icere, -iēcī, -iectum, throw away
abs. *See* **ā.**
absum, -esse, āfuī, āfutūrum, be away, be absent
ac. *See* **atque.**
accēdō, -ere, -cessī, -cessum, come near, approach
accersō. *See* **arcessō.**
accidō, -cidere, -cidī, befall, happen; **accidit,** it happens
accīdō, -cīdere, -cīdī, -cīsum, cut into
accipiō, -ere, -cēpī, -ceptum, take, receive, accept
aciēs, -ēī, *f.*, sharp edge, keenness, line of battle
ācriter, *adv.,* keenly, fiercely
ad, *prep.* with *acc.*, to, up to, near to
addō, -dere, -didī, -ditum, add, join
addūcō, -ere, -dūxī, -ductum, lead to, induce
adeō, -īre, -iī, -itum, go to, approach
adficiō (afficiō), -ere, -fēcī, -fectum, affect, afflict, weaken
adhaerēscō, -haerēscere, -haesī, cling to
adhibeō, -hibēre, -hibuī, -hibitum, take along, summon, admit, use, employ
adhortor, -ārī, -ātus sum, urge on, exhort
adiciō, -ere, -iēcī, -iectum, add
adigō, -igere, -ēgī, -āctum, drive to, hurl
adipīscor, adipīscī, adeptus sum, obtain
aditus, -ūs, *m.*, going to, approach
adiungō, -iungere, -iūnxī, -iūnctum, join to
adiūtor, -tōris, *m.*, assistant, helper, advocate
administer, -trī, *m.*, assistant

administrō (1), attend to, manage
admittō, -ere, -mīsī, -missum, admit, receive, let in
admodum, *adv.,* very, fully
adolēscō, -olēscere, -olēvī, -ultum, grow up
adorior, -orīrī, -ortus sum, rise against, attack
adsistō, -sistere, astitī, stand
adsum, -esse, -fuī, -futūrum, be near, be present, assist
adulēscēns, -centis, *m. and f.,* young man or woman
adventus, -ūs, *m.*, approach, arrival
adversus, *prep.* with *acc.,* toward, facing; against
advolō (1), fly to, hasten to
aedificium, aedificī, *n.*, building
aeger, -gra, -grum, sick, weak
aegrē, *adv.,* with difficulty, hardly, scarcely
aes, aeris, *n.*, bronze
aestās, -tātis, *f.,* summer
aestimātiō, -tionis, *f.,* valuation, worth
aestus, -ūs, *m.*, heat, tide
afficiō. *See* **adficiō.**
afflictō (1), dash against, wreck
affutūrus. *See* **adsum.**
ager, agrī, *m.*, field, farm
aggregō (1), collect, join
agmen, -minis, *n.*, army, army column
agō, -ere, ēgī, āctum, drive, lead, do, act; *of time or life,* pass, spend; **grātiās agere** *with dat.,* thank, give thanks to
alacer, -cris, -cre, lively, eager, spirited
alacritās, -tātis, *f.,* liveliness, eagerness
aliēnus, -a, -um, belonging to another (*cf.* **alius**), foreign, strange, alien
aliquī, aliqua, aliquod, *indef. pronominal adj.,* some

81

aliquis, aliquid (*gen.* alicuius; *dat.* alicui), *indef. pron.*, someone, somebody, something
aliter, *adv.*, otherwise
alius, alia, aliud, other, another; alii ... alii, some ... others
alter, -era, -erum, the other (of two), second
altitūdō, -dinis, *f.*, height, depth
altus, -a, -um, high, deep
ambactus, -ī, *m.*, retainer, dependent
ambō, -ae, -ō, both
amentum, -ī, *n.*, thong, strap (for hurling javelins)
amīcitia, -ae, *f.*, friendship
amīcus, -a, -um, friendly
amīcus, -ī, *m.*, (male) friend
āmittō, -ere, -mīsī, -missum, lose, let go
amplē, *adv.*, fully, largely
an, *adv. and conj.* introducing the second part of a double question (see utrum), or; used alone, or, can it be that
ancora, -ae, *f.*, anchor
angustē, *adv.*, closely, narrowly
angustus, -a, -um, narrow, limited
anima, -ae, *f.*, soul, spirit
animadvertō, -vertere, -vertī, -versum, turn one's mind toward, notice
animal, -mālis, *n.*, a living creature, animal
animus, -ī, *m.*, soul, spirit, mind; animī, -ōrum, high spirits, pride, courage
annus, -ī, *m.*, year
annuus, -a, -um, of a year, for a year
ante, *prep.* with *acc.*, before (*in place or time*), in front of; *adv.*, before, previously
antecursor, -ōris, *m.*, scout
anteferō, -ferre, -tulī, -lātum, prefer, place before
apertus, -a, -um, open, unprotected, exposed
appellō (1), speak to, address (as), call, name
appellō, -pellere, -pulī, -pulsum, drive to, bring to land
appropinquō (1) *with dat.*, approach, draw near to
apud, *prep. with acc.*, among, in the presence of, at the house of

aqua, -ae, *f.*, water
aquila, -ae, *f.*, eagle; the eagle as a military standard
aquilifer, -ferī, *m.*, standard-bearer
arbitror, -ārī, -ātus sum, judge, think
arcessō, -sere, -sīvī, -sītum, summon, send for, invite
ārdeō, ārdēre, ārsī, be eager, be angry
argilla, -ae, *f.*, clay
āridus, -a, -um, dry; āridum, -ī, *n.*, dry land, shore
arma, -ōrum, *n.*, arms, weapons
armāmenta, -ōrum, *n.*, equipment, implements, rigging
armātus, -a, -um, armed
armō (1), equip
arripiō, -ripere, -ripuī, -reptum, seize
ars, artis, *f.*, art, skill
artificium, artificī, *n.*, art, trick
ascendō, -scendere, -scendī, -scēnsum, climb up, scale
ascēnsus, -ūs, *m.*, way up, approach
ascīscō, -sciscere, -scīvī, -scītum, receive in alliance, receive, accept
asper, -era, -erum, rough, difficult, harsh
at, *conj.*, but; but, mind you; but, you say; *a more emotional adversative than* sed
atque *or* ac, *conj.*, and, and also, and even
attexō, -texere, -texuī, -textum, weave on, add, join
attingō, -tingere, -tigī, -tāctum, touch on, reach, extend to
attribuō, -uere, -uī, -ūtum, assign, assign to
auctor, -tōris, *m.*, increaser; author, originator
auctōritās, -tātis, *f.*, authority
audacter, *adv.*, boldly, courageously
audeō, -ēre, ausus sum, dare
audiō, -īre, -īvī, -ītum, hear, listen to
augeō, augēre, auxī, auctum, increase
aurīga, -ae, *m.*, charioteer
aut, *conj.*, or; aut ... aut, either ... or
autem, *postpositive conj.*, however; moreover
auxilior, -ārī, -ātus sum, help, aid
auxilium, auxilī, *n.*, help, aid
āvertō, -ere, -vertī, -versum, turn away, avert

balteus, -ī, *m.,* belt
barbarus, -a, -um, foreign, rude, uncivilized
bellō (1), wage war, fight
bellum, -ī, *n.,* war
beneficium, -iī, *n.,* benefit, kindness, favor
benevolentia, -ae, *f.,* good will, kindness
biennium, biennī, *n.,* a period of two years
bipertītō, *adv.,* in two parts, in two divisions
bonus, -a, -um, good, kind. *(compar.* **melior;** *superl.* **optimus.)**
brevis, -e, short, small, brief

cadō, -ere, cecidī, cāsūrum, fall
caedēs, -dis, *f.,* killing, slaughter
caelestis, -e, heavenly, celestial
caespes, -pitis, *m.,* turf, sod
calamitās, -tātis, *f.,* misfortune, disaster
capiō, -ere, cēpī, captum, take, capture, seize, get
captīvus, -ī, *m.,* captive, prisoner
carrus, -ī, *m.,* cart
castra, -ōrum, *n.,* camp
cāsus, -ūs, *m.,* accident, chance
catēna, -ae, *f.,* chain
causa, -ae, *f.,* cause, reason; case, situation; **causā** *with a preceding gen.,* for the sake of, on account of
cēdō, -ere, cessī, cessum, go, withdraw; yield to, submit, grant
celeritās, -tātis, *f.,* speed, swiftness
celeriter, *adv.,* swiftly, quickly
centum, *indecl. adj.,* a hundred
centuriō, -ōnis, *m.,* centurion
certāmen, -tāminis, *n.,* battle, contest, strife
certē, *adv.,* certainly
certus, -a, -um, definite, sure, certain, reliable
cēterī, -ae, -a, the remaining, the rest, the other
cibāria, -ōrum, *n.,* food, provisions, supplies
cingō, cingere, cīnxī, cīnctum, surround
circiter, *adv.* and *prep. with acc.,* around, about, near
circuitus, -ūs, *m.,* way around, circuitous path

circum, *prep. with acc.,* around, about, near
circumcīdō, -cīdere, -cīdī, -cīsum, cut around, cut out
circumdō, -dare, -dedī, -datum, build around, surround
circumsistō, -sistere, -stetī or **-stitī,** stand around, surround
circumspiciō, -spicere, -spexī, -spectum, look around, consider, examine
circumveniō, -venīre, -vēnī, -ventum, come around, surround, deceive
cito, *adv.,* quickly, **-datum,** build around, surround
cīvitās, -tātis, *f.,* state, citizenship
clam, *adv.,* secretly
clamitō (1), shout
clāmor, -ōris, *m.,* battle cry
clārus, -a, -um, clear, bright; renowned, famous, illustrious
cliēns, -ntis, *m.,* dependent, subject
coactū, *abl.* of **coactus,** by compulsion
coemō, -emere, -ēmī, -ēmptum, buy up
coepī, coepisse, coeptum *(defective verb; pres. system supplied by* **incipiō),** began
cognōscō, -ere, -nōvī, -nitum, become acquainted with, learn, recognize; *in perf. tenses,* know
cōgō, -ere, coēgī, coāctum, drive or bring together, force, compel
cohors, -hortis, *f.,* cohort, legionary unit
cohortātiō, -tiōnis, *f.,* encouragement, exhortation
cohortor, -ārī, -ātus sum, encourage, exhort
colligō, -ere, -lēgī, -lēctum, gather together, collect
collocō (1), place, put, arrange
colloquium, colloquī, conference, parley
colloquor, -loquī, -locūtus sum, talk with, confer with, converse
colō, -ere, coluī, cultum, cultivate; cherish
combūrō, -būrere, -bussī, -būstum, burn, destroy by fire
commeātus, -ūs, *m.,* voyage, trip, supplies
commemorō (1), remind, relate, mention
commendō (1), entrust, recommend

commeō (1), go to and fro
comminus, *adv.*, hand to hand
committō, -ere, -mīsī, -missum,
  entrust, commit
commodē, *adv.*, easily, conveniently,
  advantageously, easily
commodus, -a, -um, advantageous,
  fitting, advisable,
commūnicō (1), share with, join with,
  bestow
commūnis, -e, common, general, of or
  for the community
comparō (1), prepare, acquire
comparō (1), match, compare
comperiō, -perīre, -perī, -pertum,
  learn, find out, detect
compleō, -plēre, -plēvī, -plētum, fill,
  fill full
complūrēs, -a *or* **ia,** several, many, very
  many
comportō (1), bring together, collect,
  bring
comprehendō, -ere, -hendī, -hēnsum,
  grasp, seize, arrest; comprehend,
  understand
concēdō, -ere, -cessī, -cessum, yield,
  grant, concede
concīdō, -cīdere, -cīdī, -cīsum, cut to
  pieces, kill
conciliō (1), win over, secure
concilium, -iī, *n.*, council
concitō (1), rouse, excite
conclāmō (1), shout, cry out
concurrō, -currere, -cucurrī *or* **-currī,**
  -cursum, run together, rush, charge
concursō (1), rush about
concursus, -ūs, *m.*, running together,
  meeting, charge
condiciō, -ciōnis, *f.*, agreement,
  proposition, state
condūcō, -dūcere, -dūxī, -ductum, lead
  together, collect, hire
cōnferō, -ferre, contulī, collātum,
  bring together, compare; **sē cōnferre,**
  betake oneself, go
cōnfertus, -a, -um, crowded together,
  in close order
cōnfestim, *adv.*, Immediately, at once
cōnficiō, -ficere, -fēcī, -fectum, do
  thoroughly, complete, make
cōnfīdō, -ere, -fīsus sum, have
  confidence in, believe confidently,
  be confident

cōnfinium, cōnfinī, *n.*, boundary
cōnfirmō (1), strengthen, establish,
  settle, affirm
cōnfiteor, -ērī, -fessus sum, confess
cōnflagrō (1), be on fire, burn
cōnflictō (1), assail
coniciō, -ere, -iēcī, -iectum, throw,
  hurl, put with force; put together,
  conjecture
coniungō, -iungere, -iūnxī, -iūnctum,
  join together, unite, connect
coniūrātiō, -ōnis, *f.*, conspiracy
cōnor, -ārī, -ātus sum, try, attempt
cōnscendō, -scendere, -scendī,
  -scēnsum, mount, embark on
cōnscīscō, -scīscere, -scīvī, -scītum,
  decree, resolve on
cōnscrībō, -scrībere, -scrīpsī, -scrīptum,
  write together, enroll, enlist
cōnsecrātus, -a, -um, sacred
cōnsentiō, -sentīre, -sēnsī, -sēnsum,
  agree with, unite with
cōnsequor, -sequī, -secūtus sum,
  overtake, attain, acquire
cōnsīdō, -sīdere, -sēdī, -sessum, sit
  down, halt, encamp
cōnsilium, -iī, *n.*, counsel, advice,
  plan, purpose; judgment, wisdom
cōnsistō, -ere, -stitī, stitum, take a
  position, stand, halt; with **in,** depend
  on
cōnspiciō, -spicere, -spexī, -spectum,
  catch sight of, behold, perceive
cōnspicor, -ārī, -ātus sum, catch sight
  of, perceive, see
cōnstīpō (1), press together
cōnstituō, -stituere, -stituī, -stitūtum,
  station, point, appoint, decide
cōnstō, -āre, -stitī, -stātūrum, with **ex,**
  consist of; **cōnstat,** it is agreed;
  certain
cōnsuēscō, -ere, -suēvī, -suētum,
  become accustomed
cōnsuētūdō, -dinis, *f.*, custom, habit,
  mode of life
cōnsul, -sulis, *m.*, consul
cōnsulō, -ere, -suluī, -sultum, look out
  for, have regard for
cōnsultum, -ī, *n.*, decree
cōnsūmō, -ere, -sūmpsī, -sūmptum,
  use up, consume
cōnsurgō, -surgere, -surrēxī,
  -surrēctum, rise

contabulō (1), build over, cover
contāgiō, -giōnis, *f.,* touching, contact
contemptiō, -tiōnis, *f.,* contempt
contendō, -ere, -tendī, -tentum, strive, struggle, contend, hasten
contentiō, -tiōnis, *f.,* effort, strife, struggle
contentus, -a, -um, contented
contestor, -ārī, -ātus sum, call to witness, bring an action
contexō, -texere, -texuī, -textum, weave together, bind together, fashion
continēns, -ntis, continuous, unbroken
continenter, *adv.,* continuously, without interruption
contineō, -ēre, -tinuī, -tentum, hold together, keep, enclose, restrain, contain
contingō, -ere, -tigī, -tāctum, touch closely, befall, fall to one's lot
continuus, -a, -um, successive, in succession
contrā, *prep.* with *acc.,* against
contrōversia, -ae, *f.,* rivalry, dispute
contumēlia, -ae, *f.,* insult, indignity
convallis, -lis, *f.,* valley, ravine
conveniō, -venīre, -vēnī, -ventum, come together, assemble
conventus, -ūs, *m.,* assembly, court
convertō, -ere, -vertī, -versum, turn around, cause to turn
coörior, -orīrī, -ortus sum, arise, break out
cōpia, -ae, *f.,* abundance, supply; **cōpiae, -ārum,** supplies, troops, forces
cor, cordis, *n.,* heart
cotīdiānus, -a, -um, daily, usual
cōtīdiē, *adv.,* daily, every day
crātēs, -tis, *f.,* wicker-work, hurdle
crēber, -bra, -brum, thick, frequent, numerous
crēdō, -dere, -didī, -ditum, believe, suppose, think
crēdō, -ere, crēdidī, crēditum, believe, trust, *with dat*
cremō (1), burn
cruciātus, -ūs, *m.,* torture, punishment
culpa, -ae, *f.,* fault, blame
cultus, -us, *m.,* cultivation, civilization
cum, *conj., with subjunct.,* when, since, although; *with indic.,* when

cum, *prep.* with *abl.,* with
cūnctor (1), delay
cupidē, *adv.,* eagerly
cupiditās, -tātis, *f.,* desire, longing, passion; cupidity, avarice
cupidus, -a, -um, desirous, eager, fond; with *gen.,* desirous of, eager for
cūra, -ae, *f.,* care, attention
cūrō (1), care for, attend to; heal, cure; take care
currus, -ūs, *m.,* chariot
cursus, -ūs, *m.,* running, race; course

damnō (1), condemn
dē, *prep. with abl.,* down from, from; concerning, about
dēbeō, -ēre, -uī, -itum, owe, ought, must, should
dēcēdō, -cēdere, -cessī, -cessum, go away, withdraw, die
decem, ten
dēcernō, -ere, -crēvī, -crētum, decide, settle, decree
decimus, -a, -um, tenth
dēclīvis, -e, sloping; **dēclīvia, -ōrum,** *n.,* slopes, declivities
dēdecus, -coris, *n.,* dishonor, disgrace
dēdō, -dere, -didī, -ditum, give up, surrender, devote
dēdūcō, -dūcere, -dūxī, -ductum, lead down, lead away
dēfectiō, -tiōnis, *f.,* desertion, revolt
dēfendō, -ere, -fendī, -fēnsum, ward off, defend, protect
dēfēnsor, -sōris, *m.,* defender, guard
dēferō, -ferre, -tulī, -lātum, bring down, carry away
dēficiō, -ere, -fēcī, -fectum, fail
dēfīgō, -fīgere, -fīxī, -fīxum, drive in, fasten in
dēfugiō, -fugere, -fūgī, flee, flee from, avoid
dēiciō, -icere, -iēcī, -iectum, throw down, rout, destroy
dēiectus, -ūs, *m.,* descent, slope
deinceps, *adv.,* one after the other, in turn, in succession
deinde, *adv.,* thereupon, next, then
dēlīberō (1), consider, deliberate
dēligō (1), bind, fasten
dēligō, -ligere, -lēgī, -lēctum, choose, select, pick out

dēlitēscō, -litēscere, -lituī, hide
oneself, lie in wait, ambush

dēmetō, -metere, -messuī, -messum,
reap

dēmigrō (1), move from, move away,
depart

dēmittō, -ere, -mīsī, -missum, let
down, lower

dēmō, dēmere, dēmpsī, dēmptum, take
away, take

dēmōnstrō (1), point out, show,
demonstrate

dēmum, adv., at length, finally

dēpellō, -pellere, -pulī, -pulsum, drive
away

dēpōnō, -ere, -posuī, -positum, put
down, lay aside

dēprehendō, -prehendere, -prehendī,
-prehēnsum, seize, surprise

dēscendō, -scendere, -scendī,
-scēnsum, come down, descend

dēserō, -serere, -seruī, -sertum, leave,
desert, abandon

dēsiliō, -silīre, -siluī, -sultum, leap
down, dismount

dēspērātiō, -tiōnis, f., hopelessness,
despair

dēspērātus, -a, -um, hopeless,
desperate

dēsum, deesse, dēfuī, be wanting, be
lacking

dēturbō (1), drive off

deus, -ī, m. (nom. pl. deī or dī, dat. and
abl. pl. dīs), god

dēvehō, -vehere, -vexī, -vectum, carry
away, remove

dēvexus, -a, -um, sloping; dēvexa,
-ōrum, n., slopes

dēvoveō, -vovēre, -vōvī, -vōtum, vow,
devote

dexter, -tra, -trum, right, righthand

dīcō, -ere, dīxī, dictum, say, tell,
speak; call, name

dictiō, -ōnis, f., speaking, pleading

dictum, -ī, n., saying, word, command

diēs, -ēī, m., day

differō, -ferre, distulī, dīlātum, bear
different ways, scatter, spread out,
delay

difficilis, -e, hard, difficult, troublesome

difficultās, -tātis, f., difficulty, trouble

diffīdō, -fīdere, -fīsus sum, distrust,
despair of

dignitās, -tātis, f., merit, prestige, dignity

dīiūdicō (1), decide

dīligenter, adv., diligently

dīligō, -ere, dīlēxī, dīlēctum, esteem,
love

dīmicō (1), fight, contend

dīmittō, -ere, -mīsī, -missum, send
away, dismiss

discēdō, -ere, -cessī, -cessum, go away,
depart

disciplīna, -ae, f., training, discipline

discō, -ere, didicī, learn

dispergō, -spergere, -spersī, -spersum,
scatter, disperse

dispōnō, -pōnere, -posuī, -positum,
distribute, station

disputātiō, -ōnis, f., discussion

disputō (1), discuss

dissēnsiō, -ōnis, f., disagreement,
dissension

dissentiō, -īre, -sēnsī, -sēnsum,
disagree, differ

distribuō, -tribuere, -tribuī, -tribūtum,
divide, assign

diū, adv., for a long time, long

dīves, gen. dīvitis or dītis, rich

dīvidō, -videre, -vīsī, -vīsum, divide,
separate

dīvīnus, -a, -um, divine, sacred

dō, dare, dedī, datum, give, offer

doceō, -ēre, -uī, doctum, teach

dolor, -lōris, m., pain, grief

dominus, -ī, m., master, lord

domus, -ūs (-ī), f., house, home; domī,
at home; domum, (to) home; domō,
from home

dōs, dōtis, f., dowry

dubitātiō, -ōnis, f., doubt, hesitation

dubitō (1), doubt, hesitate

dubius, -a, -um, doubtful, uncertain

dūcō, -ere, dūxī, ductum, lead;
consider, regard; prolong

dum, conj., while, as long as; at the
same time that; until

duo, duae, duo, two

duodecim, twelve

dūrus, -a, -um, hard, harsh, rough, stern,
unfeeling, hardy, tough, difficult

dux, ducis, m., leader, guide, commander, general

ē. See ex.

ēdiscō, -discere, -didicī, learn by heart

ēdūcō, -ere, -dūxī, -ductum, lead out
effēminō (1), make effeminate, weaken
efferō, -ferre, extulī, ēlātum, carry out;
bury; lift up, exalt
efficiō, -ere, -fēcī, -fectum, accomplish, perform, bring about, cause
effugiō, -ere, -fūgī, -fugitūrum, flee
from, flee away, escape
ego, meī, I
ēgredior, -ī, -gressus sum, go out, depart
ēlābor, -lābī, -lāpsus sum, slip, away,
escape
ēmittō, -mittere, -mīsī, -missum, send
forth, let go, hurl
enim, postpositive conj., for, in fact,
truly
ēnūntiō (1), announce, report, reveal
eō, īre, iī (or īvī), itum, go
eōdem, adv., to the same place, to the
same purpose
epistula, -ae, f., letter, epistle
eques, -itis, m., horseman, cavalryman
equester, -tris, -tre, of cavalry,
equestrian
equitātus, -ūs, m., cavalry
equus, -ī, m., horse
ēripiō, -ere, -ripuī, -reptum, snatch
away, take away, rescue
errō (1), wander; err, go astray, make a
mistake, be mistaken
essedārius, -dārī, m., fighter from a
chariot
essedum, -ī, n., war chariot
et, conj., and; even (=etiam); et . . . et,
both . . . and
etiam, adv., even, also
etsī, conj., even if (et-sī), although
ēveniō, -īre, -vēnī, -ventum, come out,
turn out, happen
ēventus, -ūs, m., outcome, result
ex or ē, prep with abl., out of, from
within, from; by reason of, on
account of; following cardinal
numerals, of
exāminō (1), weigh, examine
exaudiō, -īre, -īvī, -itum, hear clearly
excēdō, -cēdere, -cessī. -cessum, go
out, go away, depart
excellō, -cellere, -celluī, -celsum,
raise, surpass
excipiō, -ere, -cēpī, -ceptum, take out,
except; take, receive, capture
excitō (1), set in motion, build, rouse

excōgitō (1), think out, devise
excruciō (1), torture
exeō, -īre, -īvī or -iī, -itum, go out, go
forth, withdraw
exercitātiō, -ōnis, f., practice, training
exercitus, -ūs, m., army
exhauriō, -haurīre, -hausī, -haustum,
draw out, take out
exiguitās, -tātis, f., smallness,
scantiness, small number
exīstimātiō, -tiōnis, f., opinion,
judgment,
exīstimō (1), think, judge, suppose
exitus, -ūs, m., way out, outcome, issue
expedītus, -a, -um, unencumbered,
light-armed
expellō, -ere, -pulī, -pulsum, drive out,
expel, banish
explōrō (1), search out, ascertain
exsequor, -sequī, -secūtus sum, follow
up, maintain, enforce
exsistō, -sistere, -stitī, stand forth,
appear, arise
exspectō (1), look for, expect, await
exstinguō, -ere, -stīnxī, -stīnctum,
extinguish
exstruō, -struere, -strūxī, -strūctum,
pile up, rear, build
extrēmus, -a, -um, outermost, last,
extreme
exūrō, -ūrere, -ussī, -ūstum, burn up

facile, adv., easily
facilis, -e, easy; agreeable, affable
facinus, -noris, n., evil deed, crime
faciō, -ere, fēcī, factum, make, do,
accomplish; passive, fīō, fierī, factus
sum
factum, -ī, n., deed, act, achievement
facultās, -tātis, f., ability, skill,
opportunity, means
falsus, -a, -um, false, deceptive
falx, falcis, f., sickle, hook shaped like
a sickle
fāma, -ae, f., rumor, report; fame,
reputation
famēs, famis, f., hunger, starvation
familia, -ae, f., household, family
familiāris, -e, referring to the family,
private
fās (indecl.), n., right, sacred duty; fās
est, it is right, fitting, lawful
fēliciter, adv., happily

femur, femoris or **feminis,** *n.,* thigh
ferē, *adv.,* almost, nearly, generally
ferō, ferre, tulī, lātum, bear, carry, bring, endure
ferrāmentum, -i, *n.,* iron tool
ferrum, -ī, *n.,* iron, sword
fervefaciō, -facere, -fēcī, -factum, make hot, heat
ferveō, fervēre, be hot
fidēs, -eī, *f.,* faith, trust, trustworthiness, fidelity; promise, guarantee, protection
figūra, -ae, *f.,* form, shape
fīlia, -ae, *f.* (*dat. and abl. pl.* **filiābus**), daughter
fīlius, -iī, *m.,* son
fīniō, -īre, -īvī, -ītum, bound, limit, measure
fīnis, -is, *m.,* end, limit, boundary; purpose; **fīnēs, -ium** (boundaries), territory
fīnitimus, -a, -um, bordering on, neighboring
fīō, fierī, factus sum, occur, happen; become, be made, be done
firmiter, *adv.,* solidly
firmus, -a, -um, firm, strong; reliable
flamma, -ae, *f.,* flame, fire
flectō, flectere, flexī, flexum, bend, turn
flētus, -ūs, *m.,* weeping
flō (1), blow
flūctus, -ūs, *m.,* billow, wave
flūmen, -minis, *n.,* river
fluō, -ere, flūxī, flūxum, flow
forte, *adv.,* by chance
fortis, -e, strong, brave
fortiter, *adv.,* bravely
fortūna, -ae, *f.,* fortune, luck
fossa, -ae, *f.,* ditch, trench
frangō, frangere, frēgī, frāctum, break, wreck, shatter
frāter, -tris, *m.,* brother
fremitus, -ūs, *m.,* uproar, noise
frūctus, -ūs, *m.,* fruit; profit, benefit, enjoyment
frūmentārius, -a, um, pertaining to grain, productive
frūmentum, -ī, *n.,* grain; **frūmenta,** crops of grain
fuga, -ae, *f.,* flight
fugiō, fugere, fūgī, fugitūrus, flee, flee from, avoid

fūmus, -ī, *m.,* smoke
funda, -ae, *f.,* sling
fundō, fundere, fūdī, fūsum, pour, throw, scatter, rout
fūnis, fūnis, *m.,* rope, cable
fūnus, -neris, *n.,* funeral, obsequies
fūrtum, -ī, *n.,* theft

gaudeō, gaudēre, gāvīsus sum, be glad, rejoice
gēns, gentis, *f.,* clan, race, nation, people
genus, generis, *n.,* origin; kind, type, sort, class
gerō, -ere, gessī, gestum, carry; carry on, manage, conduct, wage, accomplish, perform
gladius, -iī, *m.,* sword
glāns, glandis, *f.,* acorn, bullet thrown from a sling
glōria, -ae, *f.,* glory, fame
grātia, -ae, *f.,* gratitude, favor; **grātiās agere** with *dat.,* to thank
grātus, -a, -um, pleasing, agreeable; grateful
gravis, -e, heavy, weighty; serious, important; severe, grievous
graviter, *adv.,* heavily, seriously

habeō, -ēre, -uī, -itum, have, hold, possess; consider, regard
hasta, -ae, *f.,* spear
hērēditās, -tātis, *f.,* inheritance
hībernus, -a,-us, winter, wintry; **hīberna, -ōrum,** *n.,* winter quarters
hic, haec, hoc, *demonstrative adj. and pron.,* this, the latter; *at times weakened to* he, she, it, they
hīc, *adv.,* here
hiemō, (1), winter, pass the winter
hiems, hiemis, *f.,* winter, the stormy season, storm
hinc, *adv.,* hence, from here
homō, hominis, *m.,* human being, man
honestus, -a, -um, honored, honorable
honor, -nōris, *m.,* honor, esteem; public office
hōra, -ae, *f.,* hour, time
hortor, -ārī, -ātus sum, urge, encourage
hospitium, hospitī, *n.,* guest-friendship, friendship
hostis, -is, *m.,* an enemy (of the state); **hostēs, -ium,** the enemy

hūc, *adv.*, hither, here, to this place
hūmānitās, -tātis, *f.*, kindness, refinement
humilis, -e, lowly, humble
humilitās, -tātis, *f.*, lowness, insignificance

iaceō, -ēre, -uī, lie; lie prostrate; lie dead
iaciō, -ere, iēcī, iactum, throw, hurl
iaculum, -ī, *n.*, dart, javelin
iam, *adv.*, now, already, soon
ibi, *adv.*, there
īdem, eadem, idem, the same
idōneus, -a, -um, suitable, fit, appropriate
Īdūs, Īduum, *f. pl.*, the Ides
ignis, -is, *m.*, fire
ignōbilis, -e, unknown, obscure
ignoscō, -noscere, -nōvī, -nōtum, pardon, forgive, excuse
ignōtus, -a, -um, unknown
ille, illa, illud, *demonstrative adj. and pron.*, that, the former; the famous; *at times weakened to* he, she, it, they
illigō (inligō) (1), bind, fasten
illūstris, -e (inlūstris), illustrious, distinguished
immānis, -e, monstrous, huge, immense
immolō (1), sacrifice
immortālis, -e, not subject to death, immortal
immūnitās, -tātis, *f.*, freedom from taxes, Immunity
impedīmentum, -ī, *n.*, hindrance, impediment
impediō, -īre, -īvī, -ītum, impede, hinder, prevent
impellō, -ere, -pulī, -pulsum, urge on, impel
impendeō, -ēre, hang over, threaten, be imminent
imperātor, -tōris, *m.*, general, commander-in-chief, emperor
imperītus, -a, -um, inexperienced, unskilled, unacquainted
imperium, -iī, *n.*, power to command, supreme power, authority, command, control
imperō (1), give orders to, command *with dat. and* ut
impetrō (1), obtain a request, accomplish
impetus, -ūs, *m.*, attack, onset, violence

impius. -a, -um, impious
importō (1), carry in, import
imprōvīsō, *adv.*, unexpectedly
imprūdentia, -ae, *f.*, lack of foresight, carelessness, ignorance
impulsus, -ūs, *m.*, impulse, instigation
in, *prep.*with *abl.*, in, on; with *acc.*, into, toward, against
incendium, incendī, *n.*, fire, burning
incendō, -cendere, -cendī, -cēnsum, set fire to, burn
incertus, -a, -um, uncertain, unsure, doubtful
incidō, -cidere, -cidī, fall upon, fall in with, happen
incīdō, -cīdere, -cīdī, -cīsum, cut into
incipiō, -ere, -cēpī, -ceptum, begin, commence
incitō (1), urge on, excite, drive forward
incolō, -colere, -coluī, inhabit, live, dwell
incolumis, -e, safe, unharmed
incommodē, *adv.* inconveniently, unfortunately
incommodum, -ī, *n.*, inconvenience, injury, disaster
incrēdibilis, -e, incredible
inde, *adv,* thence, from that place, then
indicium, indicī, *n.*, information, evidence
indignus, -a, -um, unworthy
indūcō, -ere, -dūxī, -ductum, lead in, introduce, induce
inferior, -ius, *comparative of* inferus *(not used by Caesar)*, lower, lower part of
īnferō, -ferre, intulī, illātum, bring in, bring upon, inflict
infimus *or* imus, *superlative of* inferus *(not used by Caesar)*, lowest, lowest part of
inimīcus, -ī, *m.*, (personal) enemy
inīquus, -a, -um, unequal, unfair, unjust
initium, -iī, *n.*, beginning, commencement
initus, -a, -um, at the beginning
iniūria, -ae, *f.*, injustice, injury, wrong
iniussū, *defective noun, abl. sing. only, m.*, without the order of, without orders

innocentia, -ae, *f.*, blamelessness, integrity

inopia, -ae, *f.*, lack, want, short supply

inquam. *See* inquit.

inquit, *defective verb*, he says, *placed after one or more words of a direct quotation; other forms:* inquam, I say, inquis, you say

īnsequor, -sequī, -secūtus sum, follow up, pursue

īnsidiae, -ārum, *f. pl.*, ambush, plot, treachery

īnsinuō (1), push in

īnsistō, -sistere, -stitī, stand upon, stand, keep one's footing

īnstituō, -ere, -stituī, -stitūtum, establish, institute

īnstitūtum, -ī, *n.*, arrangement, plan, custom

īnstō, -stāre, -stitī, press on, be near, approach

īnstrūmentum, -ī, *n.*, equipment

īnsuēfactus, -a, -um, trained, well-trained

īnsula, -ae, *f.*, island

intellegō, -ere, -lēxī, -lēctum, understand

inter, *prep. with acc.*, between, among

intercēdō, -cēdere, -cessī, -cessum, go between, lie between, exist

intercipiō, -cipere, -cēpī, -ceptum, cut off, capture

interclūdō, -clūdere, -clūsī, -clūsum, cut off, shut off, blockade

interdīcō, -dīcere, -dīxī, -dictum, forbid, exclude

intereā, *adv.*, meanwhile

intereō,-īre, -iī, die, be killed

interficiō, -ere, -fēcī, -fectum, kill, murder

interim, *adv.*, meanwhile, meantime

interitus, -ūs, *m.*, death

intermittō, -mittere, -mīsī, missum, place between, lie between, cease

interpōnō, -pōnere, -posuī, -positum, place between, let pass

interpres, interpretis, *m.*, interpreter

interpretor, -ārī, ātus sum, explain

intersum, -esse, -fuī, between, take part in

intrā, *prep. with acc.*, within, inside of, before

introeō, -īre, -īvī, go in, enter into

inūsitātus, -a, -um, unusual, strange

inūtilis, -e, useless

inventor, -tōris, *m.*, inventor, originator

inveterāscō, -veterāscere, -veterāvī, grow old, become established

ipse, ipsa, ipsum, *intensive pron.*, myself, yourself, himself, herself, itself, *etc.*; the very, the actual

irrumpō, -rumpere, -rūpī, -ruptum, break into, rush into

is, ea, id, *demonstrative pron. and adj.*, this, that; *personal pron.*, he, she, it

ita, *adv. used with adjs., verbs, and advs.*, so, thus

itaque, *adv.*, and so, therefore

item, *adv.*, also, likewise, in the same manner

iter, itineris, *n.*, journey; route, road

iubeō, -ēre, iussī, iussum, bid, order, command

iūdicium, -iī, *n.*, judgment, decision, opinion; trial

iūdicō (1), judge, consider

iugum, -ī, *n.*, yoke, summit of a hill or mountain

iūmentum, -ī, *n.*, beast of burden

iūrō (1), swear

iūs, iūris, *n.*, right, justice, law; iūs iūrandum, iūris iūrandī, *n.*, oath

iussū, *defective noun, abl. sing. only*, *m.*, at the command of

iūstitia, -ae, *f.*, justice, fairness

iuventūs, -tūtis, *f.*, youth

Kalendae, -ārum, *f. pl.*, the Kalends

labor, -bōris, *m.*, labor, work, toil

labōrō (1), labor; be in distress

lacessō, -ere, -īvī, -ītum, harass, attack

lacus, -ūs, *m.*, lake

laetitia, -ae, *f.*, joy

languor, languōris, *m.*, weakness, exhaustion

lapis, -pidis, *m.*, stone

lātē, *adv.*, widely, broadly; longē lātēque, far and wide

lātitūdō, -tūdinis, *f.*, width, breadth, extent

lātrōcinium, -lātrōcinī, *n.*, robbery, brigandage

lātus, -a, -um, broad, wide, extensive
latus, -teris, *n.*, side, army flank
laus, laudis, *f.*, praise, glory, fame
lēgātiō, -tiōnis, *f.*, embassy
lēgātus, -ī, *m.*, ambassador, deputy
legiō, -ōnis, *f.*, legion
lēnis, -e, smooth, gentle, kind
levis, -e, light; easy, slight, trivial
levitās, -tātis, *f.*, lightness, fickleness
levō (1), lighten, relieve
lēx, lēgis, *f.*, law, statute
līberālitās, -tātis, *f.*, generosity,
  liberality
līberī, -ōrum, *m. pl.*, (one's) children
līberō (1), free, liberate
lībertās, -tātis, *f.*, liberty, freedom
licet, licēre, licuit, *impers. with dat.
  and infin.*, it is permitted, one may
lignātiō, -tiōnis, *f.*, getting wood
lignātor, -tōris, *m.*, woodcutter
lingua, -ae, *f.*, tongue; language
littera, -ae, *f.*, a letter of the alphabet;
  litterae, -ārum, *f. pl.*, a letter
  (epistle); literature
lītus, -toris, *n.*, shore, coast
locus, -ī, *m.*, place; passage in
  literature; *pl.*, **loca, -ōrum,** *n.*,
  places, region;
locī, - ōrum, *m.*, passages in literature
longē, *adv.*, far. *See also* **latē.**
longinquus, -a, -um, far off, remote,
  distant
longitūdō, -tūdinis, *f.*, length
longus, -a, -us, long, distant, late
loquor, -ī, locūtus sum, say, speak,
  tell, talk
lōrīca, -ae, *f.*, coat of mail, fortification
lūna, -ae, *f.*, moon
lūx, lūcis, *f.*, light

magistrātus, -ūs, *m.*, magistracy,
  official
magnificus, -a, -um, magnificent,
  splendid
magnitūdō, -tūdinis, *f.*, greatness, size,
  importance
magnopere, *adv.*, greatly, exceedingly
magnus, -a, -um, large, great;
  important (*compar.* **maior;** *superl.*
  maximus)
maior. *See* **magnus.**
maiōrēs, -um, *m. pl.*, ancestors

maleficium, maleficī, *n.*, mischief,
  harm, damage
mandātum, -ī, *n.*, order, command,
  instruction
mandō (1), commit, entrust, order
maneō, -ēre, mānsī, mānsum, remain,
  stay, abide, continue
manus, -ūs, *f.*, hand; handwriting; band
mare, -is, *n.*, sea
maritimus, -a, -um, of the sea, on the sea
māteria, -ae, *f.*, timber, wood
mātrimōnium, -iī, *n.*, marriage
mātūrō (1), hasten
maximē, *adv.*, most, especially, very
maximus. *See* **magnus.**
medeor, medērī, heal, relieve
mediocris, -e, ordinary, moderate,
  mediocre
medius, -a, -um, middle; *used
  partitively,* the middle of
melior. *See* **bonus.**
membrum, -ī, *n.*, limb
memoria, -ae, *f.*, memory, recollection
mēnsis, -is, *m.*, month
mercātor, -tōris, *m.*, trader, merchant
mercātūra, -ae, *f.*, trade
meritum, -ī, *n.*, merit, service, favor
metō, metere, messuī, messum, reap
metuō, -ere, metuī, fear, dread; be
  afraid for, *with dat*
metus, -ūs, *m.*, fear, dread, anxiety
meus, -a, -um (*m. voc.* **mī**), my
mīles, mīlitis, *m.*, soldier
militāris, -e, military
mīlitia, -ae, *f.*, military service
mīlle, *indecl. adj. in sing.*, thousand;
  mīlia, -ium, *n., pl. noun,* thousands
minimē, *adv.* least, by no means
minimus. *See* **parvus.**
minor. *See* **parvus.**
minuō, -uere, -uī, -ūtum, lessen,
  diminish
missus, -ūs, *m., used only in abl. sing.*
  missū, sending
mittō, -ere, mīsī, missum, send, let go
mōbilitās, -tātis, *f.*, quickness, speed,
  fickleness
moderor, -ārī, -ātus sum, hold in
  check, control
modo, *adv.*, now, just now, only;
  modo . . . modo, at one time . . . at
  another

modus, -ī, *m.,* measure, bound, limit; manner, method; **eius modī,** of that kind, of such a kind

moenia, -ium, *n. pl.,* walls of a city

molō, -ere, -uī, -itum, grind in a mill,

moneō, -ēre, -uī, -itum, remind, warn, advise; **moneō eum ut** *with subjunct.*

mōns, montis, *m.,* mountain

morbus, -ī, *m.,* disease, sickness

morior, -ī, mortuus sum, die

moror, -ārī, -ātus sum, delay, stay, check

mors, mortis, *f.,* death

mōs, mōris, *m.,* habit, custom, manner; **mōrēs, mōrum,** habits, morals, character

moveō, -ēre, mōvī, mōtum, move, arouse, affect

mox, *adv.,* soon

multitūdō, -tūdinis, *f.,* large number, multitude

multum, *adv.,* much (*compar.* **plūs;** *superl.* **plūrimum**)

multus, -a, -um, much, many (*compar.* **plūs;** *superl.* **plūrimus**)

mundus, -ī, *m.,* the world, universe

mūniō, -īre, -īvī, -ītum, fortify, defend; build (a road)

mūnītiō, -ōnis, *f.,* fortification, works, defenses

mūnus, -neris, *n.,* service, office, function, duty; gift

mūrālis, -e, of a wall, wall

nam, *conj.,* for

namque, *conj.,* and . . . for

nancīscor, -cīscī, nactus *and* **nanctus sum,** find, obtain

nāscor, -cī, nātus sum, be born, spring forth, arise

nātālis, -is (*sc.* **diēs**), *m.,* birthday

nātiō, -ōnis, *f.,* nation, people

nātūra, -ae, *f.,* nature

nātus, -ūs, *m.,* found only in the abl. sing. **nātū**

nauta, -ae, *m.,* sailor

nāvigium, nāvigi, *n.,* vessel, boat, ship

nāvigō (1), sail, navigate

nāvis, -is, *f.,* ship

nē, *conj. with subjunct.,* that . . . not, in order that . . . not, in order not to; that; *adv. in* **nē . . . quidem,** not . . . even

-ne, *interrog.* suffix attached to the first word of a sentence, typically the verb or another word on which the question hinges, to introduce a question whose answer is uncertain.

nec. *See* **neque.**

necessāriō, *adv.,* necessarily, of necessity

necessārius, -a, -um, necessary

necesse, *indecl. adj.,* necessary, inevitable

necō (1), murder, kill

neglegō, -ere, -lēxī, -lēctum, neglect, disregard

negō (1), deny, say that . . . not

negōtium, negōtī, *n.,* business, affair, trouble, difficulty

nēmō, (nullīus), nēminī, nēminem (nūllō, -ā), *m. / f.,* no one, nobody

neque *or* **nec,** *conj.,* and not, nor; **neque . . . neque,** neither . . . nor

nēve *or* **neu,** and not, nor (*used to continue* ut *or* nē *with subjunct.*)

nihil (*indecl.*), *n.,* nothing; **nihilō minus,** nonetheless

nisi, *conj.,* if . . . not, unless, except

nōbilis, -e, well known, eminent; a man of noble rank

nōbilitās, -tātis, *f.,* fame, eminence

nocens, -ntis, guilty

noceō, -ēre, nocuī, nocitum *with dat.,* do harm to, harm, injure

noctū, *adv.,* by night

nocturnus, -a, -um, at night, by night

nōlō, nōlle, nōluī, not wish, be unwilling

nōmen, nōminis, *n.,* name

nōn, *adv.,* not

Nōnae, -ārum, *f. plur.,* the Nones

nōndum, *adv.,* not yet

nōscō, become acquainted with, learn, recognize; *in perf. tenses,* know

noster, -tra, -trum, our, ours

nōtus, -a, -um, known, familiar, well known

novitās, -tātis, *f.,* newness, strangeness

novus, -a, -um, new, strange

nox, noctis, *f.,* night

noxia, -ae, *f.*, crime, offence
nūdō (1), lay bare, expose, strip
nūllus, -a, -um, not any, no, none
num, *interrog. adv.*: (1) *introduces direct questions which expect the answer no;* (2) *introduces ind. questions and means* whether
nūmen, -inis, *n.*, will, power (of the gods)
numerus, -ī, *m.*, number
numquam, *adv.*, never
nunc, *adv.*, now, at present
nūntiō (1), announce, report, relate
nūntius, -iī, *m.*, messenger, message
nūper, *adv.*, recently
nūtus, -ūs, *m.*, nod, command

ob, *prep. with acc.*, on account of, for
obaerātus, -a, -um, in debt
obeō, -īre, -iī, -itum, go up against, meet; die
observō (1), watch, observe
obses, obsidis, *m.* / *f.*, hostage
obsideō, -sidēre, -sēdī, -sessum, besiege, beset, occupy
obsidiō, -ōnis, *f.*, siege, blockade, oppression
obtineō, -tinēre, -tinuī, -tentum, hold, occupy, secure
occāsiō, -ōnis, *f.*, occasion, opportunity
occāsus, -ūs, *m.*, falling, setting
occidō, -ere, -cidī, -cāsum (cadō, fall), fall down; die; set (*of the sun*)
occīdō, -ere, -cīdī, -cīsum (caedō, cut), cut down; kill, slay
occultō (1), conceal, hide
occultus, -a, -um, concealed, hidden, secret
occupō (1), seize
occurrō, -currere, -currī *or* -cucurrī, run against, meet, encounter
octāvus, -a, -um, eighth
officium, -iī, *n.*, duty, service
omnīnō, *adv.*, wholly, entirely, altogether
omnis, -e, every, all
onus, oneris, *n.*, burden, load
opera, -ae, *f.*, work, pains, help
opīniō, -ōnis, *f.*, notion, reputation, impression
oportet, -ēre, oportuit (*impers.*), it is necessary, proper, right

oppidum, -ī, *n.*, town, walled town
opportūnus, -a, -um, fit, suitable, advantageous, opportune
opprimō, -ere, -pressī, -pressum, suppress, overwhelm, overpower, check
oppugnātiō, -ōnis, *f.*, storming, attack, siege
oppugnō (1), fight against, attack, assault, assail
optimus. *See* bonus.
opus, operis, *n.*, a work, task; deed, accomplishment
opus, *n.*, necessity, need; opus est, there is need, it is necessary
ōra, -ae, *f.*, shore, coast
ōrātiō, -ōnis, *f.*, speech
ōrātor, -tōris, *m.*, orator, speaker
orbis, -is, *m.*, circle, orb; orbis terrārum, the world, the earth
ōrdō, ōrdinis, *m.*, rank, class, order
orior, -īrī, ortus sum, arise, begin, proceed, originate
ōrō (1), speak, plead; beg, beseech, entreat, pray
ortus, -ūs, *m.*, rising
ōs, ōris, *n.*, mouth, face
ostendō, -ere, -tendī, -tentum, exhibit, show, display
ostentō (1), display

pācātus, -a, -um, subdued, peaceful
paene, *adv.*, almost, nearly
palam, *adv.*, openly, plainly
pār, *gen.* paris, equal, like
parātus, -a, -um, ready, prepared, equipped
parcō, -ere, pepercī, parsūrum, *with dat.*, be lenient to, spare
parēns, -rentis, *m.* / *f.*, parent
pāreō, -ēre, -uī, *with dat.*, be obedient to, obey
parō (1), prepare, provide; get, obtain
pars, partis, *f.*, part, share; direction
parvus, -a, -um, small, unimportant
passus, -ūs, *m.*, pace, double step; mīlle passūs, a mile
pateō, -ēre, -uī, be open, lie open; be accessible; be evident
pater, -tris, *m.*, father
patior, -ī, passus sum, suffer, endure; permit

paucī, -ae, -a, *usually pl.*, few, a few
paucitās, -tātis, *f.*, paucity, small
number
paulātim, *adv.*, gradually, little by
little
paulō, *adv.*, a little, by a little
paulum, *adv.*, a little, somewhat
pāx, pācis, *f.*, peace
pecūnia, -ae, *f.*, money
pedes, -itis, *m.*, foot soldier; **plur.**,
infantry
pedester, -tris, -tre, on foot, referring
to foot soldiers
peditātus, -ūs, *m.*, infantry
pellō, -ere, pepulī, pulsum, strike,
push; drive out, banish
pendō, pendere, pependī, pēnsum,
weigh out, pay
per, *prep. with acc.*, through; *with*
reflexive pron., by
peragō, -agere, -ēgī, -āctum, do
thoroughly, finish
percurrō, -currere, -cucurrī *or* **-currī,**
-cursum, run through, run along
percutiō, -cutere, -cussī, -cussum,
strike through, pierce
perdiscō, -discere, -didicī, learn
thoroughly, learn by heart
perdūcō, -dūcere, -dūxī, -ductum, lead
through, conduct, convey
perendinus, -a, -um, of the day after
tomorrow
perequitō (1), ride through, ride about
perfacilis, -e, very easy
perferō, -ferre, -tulī, -lātum, bear,
endure, suffer
perficiō, -ere, -fēcī, -fectum, do
thoroughly, accomplish, bring about
perfugiō, -fugere, -fūgī, flee for refuge,
desert
perīculum, -ī, *n.*, danger, risk
perimō, -ere, -ēmī, -ēmptum, destroy
perītus, -a, -um, skilled, expert
perlegō, -legere, -lēgī, -lēctum, read
through
permaneō, -manēre, -mānsī, -mānsum,
remain, continue, abide by
permittō, -mittere, -mīsī, -missum,
entrust, permit, allow
permoveō, -movēre, -mōvī, -mōtum,
move deeply, influence, arouse
perpaucī, -ae, -a, very few

perpetuus, -a, -um, perpetual, lasting,
uninterrupted, continuous
perscrībō, -ere, -scrīpsī, -scrīptum,
write out, place on record
persēverō (1), continue, persist
perspiciō, -spicere, -spexī, -spectum,
see through, see, observe
persuādeō, -ēre, -suāsī, -suāsum,
succeed in urging, persuade, convince
perterreō, -ēre, -uī, -itum, frighten
thoroughly, terrify
pertinācia, -ae, *f.*, stubbornness
pertineō, -tinēre, -tinuī, extend,
stretch, tend to
perturbātiō, -ōnis, *f.*, disturbance,
commotion
perturbō (1), throw into confusion,
disturb
perveniō, -venīre, -vēnī, -ventum,
come to, reach, arrive
pēs, pedis, *m.*, foot
petō, petere, petīvī, petītum, seek, try
to reach, attack
pietās, -tātis, *f.*, loyalty, devotion
pīlum, -ī, *n.*, javelin, pike
pinna, -ae, *f.*, feather, battlement
plācō (1), placate, appease
plēbs, plēbis, *f.*, the common people,
populace, plebeians
plēnus, -a, -um, full, abundant,
generous
plērumque, *adv.*, generally, for the
most part, as a rule
plērusque, -raque, -rumque, *usually*
plural, very many, most
plūrimum, *adv.*, very much
plūrimus. *See* **multus.**
plūs. *See* **multus.**
poena, -ae, *f.*, penalty, punishment;
poenās dare, pay the penalty
polliceor, -licērī, -licitus sum,
promise, offer
pōnō, -ere, posuī, positum, put, place, set
pōns, pontis, *m.*, bridge
populus, -ī, *m.*, the people, a people,
nation
porrō, *adv.*, further, furthermore
porta, -ae, *f.*, gate, entrance
portō (1), carry, bring
portus, -ūs, *m.*, harbor, port
possum, posse, potuī, be able, can,
have power

post, *prep. with acc.*, after, behind;
adv. after, afterward
posteā, *adv.*, afterward
posterus, -a, -um, following; posterī,
-ōrum, *m.*, descendants
postrēmō, *adv.*, after all, finally; for
the last time
potēns, *gen.* -tentis, *pres. partic. of*
possum *as adj.*, able, powerful,
mighty, strong
potestās, -tātis, *f.*, power, ability,
opportunity
potior, -īrī, potītus sum *with gen. or
abl.*, get possession of, possess, hold
praecēdō, -cēdere, -cessī, cessum, go
before, precede, surpass
praeceps, -cipitis, headlong
praecipiō, -cipere, -cēpī, -ceptum,
anticipate, order
praeda. -ae, *f.*, booty, plunder
praedicō (1), assert, declare, claim
praeficiō, -ere, -fēcī, -fectum, put in
charge of
praemittō, -ere, -mīsī, -missum, send
ahead or forward
praemium, -iī, *n.*, reward, prize
praesēns, -ntis, present, in person
praesentia, -ae, *f.*, presence
praesertim, *adv.*, especially, particularly
praesidium, -iī, *n.*, guard, detachment,
protection
praestō, -āre, -stitī, -stitum, excel
(with dat.); exhibit, show, offer,
supply
praestō, *adv.*, present, at hand
praesum, -esse, -fuī, be at the head of,
be in charge of
praeter, *prep. with acc.*, besides,
except; beyond, past
praetereā, *adv.*, besides, moreover
praeterquam, *adv.*, other than, besides
praeūstus, -a, -um, burnt at the end
premō, -ere, pressī, pressum, press;
press hard, pursue
prīdiē, *adv.*, the day before
prīmō, *adv.*, at first, first, at the
beginning
prīmus. *See* prior.
princeps, principis, *m. / f.*, chief,
leader, prince, emperor
principātus, -ūs, *m.*, headship,
leadership

prior, prius, former, prior; prīmus, -a,
-um, first, foremost, chief, principal
prīstinus, -a, -um, ancient, former,
previous
prius, *adv.*, before, previously
prīvātus, -ī, *m.*, private citizen
prō, *prep. with abl.*, in front of, before,
on behalf of, in return for, instead
of, for, as
probō (1), approve; recommend; test
prōcēdō, -cēdere, -cessī, -cessum, go
forward, proceed
procul, *adv.*, far off, at a distance, from
afar
prōcūrō (1), care for, manage, attend to
prōcurrō, -currere, -cucurrī or -currī,
-cursum, run forward
prōdeō, -īre, -īvī or -iī, -itum, come
forward, advance
prōdō, -dere, -didī, -ditum, give up,
betray, hand down
prōdūcō, -dūcere, -dūxī, -ductum, lead
forth, lead out, prolong
proelior, -ārī, -ātus sum, fight
proelium, -iī, *n.*, battle
profectiō, -ōnis, *f.*, departure, setting out
prōficiō, -ficere, -fēcī, -fectum, effect,
accomplish, make
prōficīscor, -ī, -fectus sum, set out, start
profiteor, -fitērī, -fessus sum, promise,
offer, volunteer
prōgnātus, -a, -um, descended, sprung
prōgredior, -gredī, -gressus sum,
advance, proceed
prohibeō, -ēre, -uī, -itum, prevent,
hinder, restrain, prohibit
prōiciō, -ere, -iēcī, -iectum, throw
forward or out
proinde, *adv.*, therefore
prōnūntiō (1), proclaim, announce;
declaim; pronounce
prope, *adv.*, near, almost
prōpellō, -pellere, -pulī, -pulsum, drive
away, repel
properō (1), hasten, hurry
propinquus, -a, -um, near, neighboring
proprius, -a, -um, one's own, peculiar,
proper, personal, characteristic
propter, *prep. with acc.*, on account of,
because of
proptereā, *adv.*, on that account, on
this account

prōsequor, -sequī, -secūtus sum,
follow, pursue
prōtegō, -tegere, -tēxī, -tēctum, protect
prōvehō, -vehere, -vexī, -vectum, carry
forward; *pass.*, put out to sea, set sail
prōveniō, -venīre, -vēnī, -ventum,
come forth, grow out
prōvideō, -ēre, -vīdī, -vīsum, foresee,
provide, make provision
prōvincia, -ae, *f.*, province
proximē, *adv.*, nearest, next
proximus, -a, -um (*superl.* of propior),
nearest, next
publicē, *adv.*, publicly, as a state
pūblicus, -a, -um, of the people,
public; rēs pūblica, reī pūblicae, *f.*,
the state
puerīlis, e, of a boy, young
pugna, -ae, *f.*, fight, battle
pugnō (1), fight
pulvis, -veris, *m.*, dust
putō (1), reckon, suppose, judge, think,
imagine

quā, *adv.*, by which route, where
quadringentī, -ae, -a, four hundred
quaestiō, -ōnis, *f.*, investigation, trial
quaestor, -tōris, *m.*, Roman official; in
the army, quartermaster and
paymaster
quaestus, -ūs, *m.*, gain
quam, *adv.* and *conj.*, how, than, as
quantus, -a, -um, *inter.* and *rel.*, how
great?, how much?, as great as, as
much as
quantusvīs, -avīs, -umvīs, as great as
you wish, however great
quārē or quā rē, *adv.*, wherefore? why?;
on acount of which
quārtus, -a, -um, fourth
-que, *enclitic conj.*, and
queror, querī, questus sum, complain,
complain of, lament
quī, quae, quod, *rel. pron.*, who, which,
what, that
quī, quae, quod, *interrog. adj.*, what?
which? what kind of?; *sometimes
with exclamatory force*, what (a)!,
what sort of!
quīcumque, quaecumque, quod-
cumque, *pron. and adj.*, whoever,
whatever, whichever

quīdam, quaedam, quiddam (*pron.*) or
quoddam (*adj.*), *indef. pron. and adj.*:
as pron., a certain one or thing,
someone, something; *as adj.*, a
certain
quidem, *adv.*, indeed, at least; nē . . .
quidem, not even
quiēs, quiētis, *f.*, rest, quiet, sleep
quiētus, -a, -um, quiet, peaceful
quīn, *conj.*, why not, that not, but
that
quīndecim, fifteen
quīnquāgintā, fifty
quis, quid, *interrog. pron.*, who? what?
which?
quisnam, quaenam, quidnam,
interrog. pron., who, pray? what in
the world?
quispiam, quaepiam, quidpiam or
quodpiam, *pron. and adj.*, anyone,
anything
quisquam, quicquam, *pron.*, anyone,
anything
quisque, quaeque, quidque or
quodque, *pron. and adj.*, each one,
each person, each thing
quō, *adv.*, to which or what place,
whither, where
quō, *conj.*, in order that, that
quoad, *conj.*, as long as, until
quod, *conj.*, because
quoniam, *conj.*, since, inasmuch as
quoque, *adv.*, also, too
quot, *indecl. adj.*, how many?; as many
quotiēns, *adv.*, how often?; as often as

ratiō, -ōnis, *f.*, reckoning, account;
reason, judgment, consideration;
system, manner, method
rebelliō, -ōnis, *f.*, renewal of fighting,
revolt, uprising
recēdō, -ere, -cessī, -cessum, go back,
retire, recede
recēns, recentis, fresh, new
recessus, -ūs, *m.*, retreat, means of
retreat
recipiō, -ere, -cēpī, -ceptum, take
back, regain; admit, receive
recitō (1), read aloud, recite
recūsō (1), refuse
reddō, -ere, -didī, -ditum, give back,
return

redeō, -īre, -iī, -itum, go back, return
redigō, -igere, -ēgī, -āctum, drive back,
  reduce, make
reditiō, -ōnis, f., returning, return
reditus, -ūs, m., returning, return
redūcō, -ere, -dūxī, -ductum, lead
  back, bring back
referō, referre, rettulī, relātum, carry
  back, bring back; repeat, answer,
  report
reficiō, -ficere, -fēcī, -fectum, make
  over, repair, refresh
refugiō, -fugere, -fūgī, flee back, flee
regiō, -ōnis, f., direction, region,
  territory
regnō (1), rule, reign, be king
rēgnum, -ī, n., rule, authority,
  kingdom
regō, -ere, rēxī, rēctum, rule, guide,
  direct
regredior, -gredī, -gressus sum, come
  back, go back, return
rēiciō, -icere, -iēcī, -iectum, throw
  back, drive back, repulse
relēgō (1), banish
religiō, -ōnis, f., religious observance,
  religion, superstition
relinquō, -ere, -līquī, -lictum, leave
  behind, leave, abandon
reliquus, -a, -um, remaining, the rest of
remaneō, -ēre, -mānsī, -mānsum,
  remain, stay behind, abide, continue
remigrō (1), move back, go back
remittō, -mittere, -mīsī, -missum,
  send back, hurl back, relax
removeō, -ēre, -mōvī, -mōtum, remove
remus, -ī, m., oar
repellō, repellere, reppulī, repulsum,
  drive back, repulse
repentīnus, -a, -um, sudden, unexpected
reperiō, reperīre, repperī, repertum,
  find, discover, learn; get
reportō (1), carry back
reposcō, -poscere, demand back,
  demand
reprehendō, -prehendere, -prehendī,
  -prehēnsum, hold back, criticize,
  blame
rēs, reī, f., thing, matter, business,
  affair; rēs pūblica, reī pūblicae,
  state, commonwealth

rescindō, -scindere, -scidī, -scissum,
  cut down, tear down, destroy
reservō (1), keep back, reserve
resistō, -ere, -stitī, make a stand,
  resist, oppose
respiciō, -spicere, -spexī, -spectum,
  look back, consider, regard
respondeō, -ēre, -spondī, -spōnsum,
  answer
restituō, -ere, -stituī, -stitūtum,
  restore
retineō, -tinēre, -tinuī, -tentum, hold
  back, restrain
revertor, -ī, -vertī (perf. is act.),
  -versum, return
rīpa, -ae, f., bank of a river
rogō (1), ask, ask for; rogō eum ut, with
  subjunct., ask whether
rota, -ae, f., wheel
rūmor, -mōris, m., rumor, gossip
rūpēs, rūpis, f., cliff, rock
rūrsus, adv. again, anew, in turn

sacrificium, -iī, n., sacrifice
saepe, adv., often
sagitta, -ae, f., arrow
sagulum, -ī, military cloak
saltus, ūs, m., a wood, mountain pass
salūs, salūtis, f., health, safety;
  greeting
sānctus, -a, -um, sacred, holy
sapiō, -ere, sapīvī, have good taste;
  have good sense, be wise
satis, indecl. noun, adj., and adv.,
  enough, sufficient(ly)
satisfaciō, -facere, -fēcī, -factum,
  satisfy, give satisfaction, apologize
saucius, -a, -um, wounded
scālae, -ārum, f., ladder, scaling ladder
scapha, -ae, f., skiff, small boat
scelerātus, -a, -um, criminal, wicked,
  accursed
sciō, -īre, -īvī, -ītum, know
scrībō, -ere, scrīpsī, scrīptum, write,
  compose
scūtum, -ī, n., shield
sē, sēsē. See suī.
sed, conj., but
sēmentis, -ntis, f., sowing, planting
senātus, -ūs, m., Senate
sententia, -ae, f., feeling, thought,
  opinion, vote; sentence

sentiō, -īre, sēnsī, sēnsum, feel,
   perceive, think, experience
septentriōnēs, -um, m., the north
septimus, -a, -um, seventh
sequor, -ī, secūtus sum, follow
sermō, -mōnis, m., conversation, talk
sērō, adv., too late, late
servīlis, -e, servile, of the slaves
servitūs, -tūtis, f., servitude, slavery
servō (1), preserve, keep, save, guard
servus, -ī, m., slave
seu. See sive.
sī, conj., if
sīc, adv. (most commonly with verbs),
   so, thus
siccitās, -tātis, f., dryness, drought
sīcut, adv. and conj., as, just as, as it
   were
sīdus, -deris, n., constellation, star
signum, -ī, n., sign, signal, indication;
   seal
silva, -ae, f., forest, wood
similis, -e, similar to, like, resembling
simul, adv., at the same time, at once
simulācrum, -ī, n., likeness, image
simulātiō, -ōnis, f., pretense
sīn, conj., but if
sine, prep. with abl., without
singulāris, -e, single, one by one
singulī, -ae, -a, pl., one each, single,
   separate
sīve or seu, conj., or if
socius, -ii, m., companion, ally
sōl, sōlis, m., sun
soleō, -ēre, solitus sum, be accustomed
solvō, solvere, solvī, solūtum, loose,
   cast off, set sail
spatium, -ii, n., space, distance,
   interval
speciēs, -ēī, f., sight, appearance,
   show
spectō (1), look at, see
speculātōrius, -a, -um, spying,
   scouting
spērō (1), hope for, hope
spēs, -eī, f., hope
sponte, adv., of one's own accord,
   voluntarily
stabilitās, -tātis, f., steadiness,
   firmness
statim, adv., immediately, at once
statiō, -ōnis, f., post, guard

stīpendium, -pendī, n., tribute
stō, stāre, stetī, statum, stand, stand
   still or firm
strāmentum, -ī, n., straw, packsaddle
strepitus, -ūs, m., noise, uproar
studeō, -ēre, -uī, with dat., direct one's
   zeal to, be eager for, study
studium, -ii, n., eagerness, zeal,
   pursuit, study
sub, prep. with abl. with verbs of rest,
   with acc. with verbs of motion,
   under, up under, close to
subdūcō, -dūcere, -dūxī, -ductum, lead
   up, lead off, beach
subeō, -īre, -iī, itum, go under, suffer,
   approach
subitō, adv., suddenly
subsequor, -sequī, -secūtus sum, flow
   after, follow up, succeed
subsidium -iī, n., reserve, reinforce-
   ment, aid
subsum, -esse, be near, be at hand
subveniō, -venīre, -vēnī, -ventum,
   come under, come to the aid of
succēdō, -cēdere, -cessī, -cessum,
   come up, approach, take the place of
succendō, -cendere, -cendī, cēnsum,
   set on fire, kindle
succurrō, -ere, -currī, -cursum, run up
   under, help
sudis, sudis, f., stake
suffrāgium, -iī, n., vote
suī (sibi, sē, sē), reflexive pron. of 3rd
   pers., himself, herself, itself,
   themselves
sum, esse, fuī, futūrum, be, exist.; est,
   sunt may mean there is, there are
summittō, -mittere, -mīsī, -missum,
   let down, send as aid, help
summoveō, -movēre, -mōvī, -mōtum,
   move back, remove, repulse
sūmō, -ere, sūmpsī, sūmptum, take,
   take up, assume
sūmptuōsus, -a, -um, expensive, costly,
   superior. See superus.
superō (1), be above, have the upper
   hand, surpass, overcome, conquer
superus, -a, -um, above, upper; superī,
   -ōrum, m., the gods (compar.
   superior, -ius, higher; superl.
   suprēmus, -a, -um, last, or summus,
   -a, -um, highest)

suppetō, -petere, -petīvī *or* **-petiī, -petītum,** be at hand
supplex, -plicis, *m.* / *f.*, suppliant
suprā, *adv. and prep. with acc.*, above
suprēmus. *See* **superus.**
suscipiō, -ere, -cēpī, -ceptum, undertake
suspīciō, -ōnis, *f.*, suspicion
suspicor, -ārī, -ātus sum, suspect
sustentō (1), hold out, sustain, endure
sustineō, -ēre, -uī, -tentum, hold up, sustain, endure
suus, -a, -um, *reflexive possessive adj. of 3rd pers.*, his own, her own, its own, their own

tamen, *adv.*, nevertheless, still
tametsī, *conj.*, although, though
tandem, *adv.*, at last, finally
tantum, *adv.*, only
tantus, -a, -um, so large, so great, of such size
tegō, -ere, tēxī, tēctum, cover, hide, protect
tēlum, -ī, *n.*, dart, spear, javelin
temerārius, -a, -um, rash, reckless
temere, *adv.*, blindly, rashly, without good reason
tēmō, -mōnis, *m.*, pole of a chariot
temperō (1), control oneself, restrain from
tempestās, -tātis, *f.*, period of time, season; weather, storm
tempus, -poris, *n.*, time; occasion, ep, possess, restrain
tenuis, tenue, thin, slight, feeble
tergum, -ī, *n.*, back; **ā tergō, post tergum,** in the rear
terra, -ae, *f.*, earth, ground, land, country
terreō, -ēre, -uī, -itum, frighten, terrify
terror, -ōris, *m.*, fear, terror
tertius, -a, -um, third
testimōnium, testimōnī, *n.*, proof
testis, testis, *m.* / *f.*, witness
testūdō, -dinis, *f.*, tortoise, testudo (military tactic)
timeō, -ēre, -uī, fear, be afraid of, be afraid
timidē, *adv.*, timidly
timor, -mōris, *m.*, fear
tolerō (1), bear, endure, tolerate

tollō, -ere, sustulī, sublātum, raise, lift up; take away, remove, destroy
tormentum, -ī, *n.*, engine for hurling missiles
torreō, torrēre, torruī, tostum, roast, scorch
tot, *indecl. adj.*, that number of, so many
tōtus, -a, -um, whole, entire
trādō, -ere, -didī, -ditum, give over, surrender, hand down, transmit, teach
trāgula, -ae, *f.*, spear, javelin
trāiciō, -icere, -iēcī, -iectum, throw across, pierce
trāns, *prep. with acc.*, across
trānseō, -īre, -iī, -itum, go across, cross; pass over, ignore
trānsferō, -ferre, -tulī, -lātum, bear across, transfer, convey
trānsfīgō, -figere, -fīxī, -fixum, transfix, pierce
trānsportō (1), carry across, bring over
trepidō (1), rush about, be agitated
trēs, tria, three
tribūnus, -ī, *m.*, tribune
tribūtum, -ī, *n.*, tax, tribute
trīs. *See* **trēs.**
tū, tuī, you
tum, *adv.*, then, at that time; thereupon, in the next place
tumultus, -ūs, *m.*, uprising, disturbance
tumulus, -ī, *m.*, mound, tomb
tunc, *adv.*, then, at that time
turma, -ae, *f.*, troop, cavalry squad
turpis, -e, ugly; shameful, base, disgraceful
turpiter, *adv.*, disgracefully, shamefully
turris, turris, *f.*, tower
tūtus, -a, -um, protected, safe, secure
tuus, -a, -um, your, yours (*sing.*)

ubi, *rel. adv. and conj.*, where; when; *interrog.*, where?
ubīque, *adv.*, anywhere, everywhere
ulcīscor, -ī, ultus sum, avenge, punish for wrong done
ūllus, -a, -um, any
ulterior, ulterius, farther, more remote, beyond

ultrō, *adv.,* beyond, besides, voluntarily
ululātus, -ūs, *m.,* yell, shriek, cry
ūnā, *adv.,* together; **ūnā cum,** together with
unde, *adv.,* whence, from what or which place; from which, from whom
ūndecim, eleven
undique, *adv.,* from all sides, on all sides, everywhere
ūniversus, -a, -um, all together, whole, entire
ūnus, -a, -um, one, single, alone
urbs, urbis, *f.,* city
ūsus, -ūs, *m.,* use, experience, skill, advantage
ut, utī, *conj.;* (1) *with subjunct.,* introducing (a) *purpose,* in order that, that, to; (b) *result,* so that, that; (c) *jussive noun clauses,* to, that; (d) *fear clauses,* that . . . not); (2) *with indic.,* just as, as, when
uter, utra, utrum, either, which (of two)
uterque, utraque, utrumque, each, both
ūtor, -ī, ūsus sum, with *abl.,* use; enjoy, experience
uxor, -ōris, *f.,* wife

vacātiō, -tiōnis, *f.,* freedom from, exemption
vadum, -ī, *n.,* shallow place, ford
vagīna, -ae, *f.,* sheath, scabbard
vagor, -ārī, -ātus sum, wander, wander about, roam
valētūdō, -dinis, *f.,* health, good health, bad health
vallum, -ī, *n.,* wall of stakes, palisade, rampart
vel, *conj.,* or (*an optional alternative*)
vēlōciter, *adv.,* swiftly
veniō, -īre, vēnī, ventum, come
ventitō (1), come often
ventus, -ī, *m.,* wind
vereor, verērī, veritus sum, fear, be afraid of, dread, stand in awe of
vergō, vergere, slope, extend, lie
vērō, *adv.,* in truth, indeed, to be sure, however

versō (1), turn about, treat, deal with; as a deponent, move about, be busy, be engaged
versus, -ūs, *m.,* line, verse
vertō, -ere, vertī, versum, turn, change
vērus, -a, -um, true, real, proper
verūtum, -ī, *n.,* javelin, dart
via, -ae, *f.,* road, street, way
victima, -ae, *f.,* sacrificial offering
victor, -tōris, *m.,* victor
victōria, -ae, *f.,* victory
vīcus, -ī, *m.,* village
videō, -ēre, vīdī, vīsum, see, observe; understand; **videor, -ērī, vīsus sum,** be seen, seem, appear
vigilia, -ae, *f.,* watching, wakefulness, watch
vīmen, -minis, *n.,* twig, osier
vinciō, vincīre, vinxī, vinctum, bind
vincō, -ere, vīcī, victum, conquer, overcome
vinculum, -ī, *n.,* bond, chain
vir, virī, *m.,* man, hero
virtūs, -tūtis, *f.,* manliness, courage; excellence, virtue, character, worth
vīs, vīs, *f.,* force, power, violence; *pl.* **vīrēs, vīrium,** strength
vīta, -ae, *f.,* life, mode of life
vītō (1), avoid, shun
vīvus, -a, -um, alive, living
vix, *adv.,* hardly, scarcely, with difficulty
vocō (1), call, summon
volō, velle, voluī, wish, want, be willing, will
voluntās, -tātis, *f.,* will, wish
voveō, vovēre, vōvī, vōtum, vow
vōx, vōcis, *f.,* voice, word
vulgō, *adv.,* commonly, generally, everywhere
vulgus, -ī, *n.* (*sometimes m.*), the common people, mob, rabble
vulnerō (1), wound
vulnus, -neris, *n.,* wound
vultus, -ūs, *m.,* countenance, face

GEOGRAPHICAL INDEX

The numbers following each entry indicate, by book and chapter, the word's first appearance in our text.

INDEX OF PEOPLE

The numbers following each entry indicate, by book and chapter, the name's first appearance in our text.

CPSIA information can be obtained at www.ICGtesting.com
Printed in the USA
LVOW060121090812

293590LV00002B/1/P